Rasa

Rasa

Performing the Divine in India

Susan L. Schwartz

Columbia University Press
New York

Columbia University Press
Publishers Since 1893
New York
Chichester, West Sussex

Library of Congress Cataloging-in-Publication Data
Rasa.
p. cm.
ISBN 0–231–13144–5 (cloth) — ISBN 0–231–13145–3 (pbk.)
1. Performing arts—India.

PN2881.R29   2004
791'.0954—dc22   2003062701

Columbia University Press books are printed on
permanent and durable acid-free paper.
Printed in the United States of America
Designed by Katie Chan
c 10 9 8 7 6 5 4 3 2 1
p 10 9 8 7 6 5 4 3 2 1

To H. Daniel Smith, with gratitude

Contents

Preface

This study is intended as the third in the series of books currently including *Darśan*, by Diana Eck, and *Mantra*, by Harold Coward and David Goa. Like them, it proposes to introduce readers to basic concepts in India's long and rich religious and cultural traditions by focusing on a particular theme, in this case the theory and application of the aesthetic principle *rasa*. Readers should gain an appreciation of a sampling of the historical and textual traditions pertaining to *rasa*, and of how this principle has been applied in a range of Indian performance traditions. The primary goal is to explicate the origins of Indian aesthetics in religious belief and practice, to articulate the religious sensibility responsible for those origins, and to begin to chart the difficult waters of change that characterize Indian aesthetics in respect to religion currently.

Within India, the issue of religion's role in the country's prolific arts communities is controversial. Elsewhere, the religious roots of these arts are often ignored. While many outside of India find the images, sounds, and practices of Indian performing arts compelling and endeavor to incorporate them into the "global" repertoire, the religious origins and contexts of those traditions often seem to be lost in the process. Misrepresentation is a real and palpable danger in this context. This book attempts to articulate the meaning and significance of *rasa* in order to provide a perspective from which performance traditions in India, both classical and nonclassical, may be understood.

As is inevitably the case in an effort to distill from a huge library of material a cogent and accessible introductory text, much more has been left out than included. I have designed this volume to serve a variety of interested readers, from students of religion and theater to those with an interest in Indian philosophy, without overloading the text with the jargon of any one of these fields of study or with vocabulary from Sanskrit, Tamil, Telegu, or other South Asian languages that would prove difficult for the introductory reader to understand. My purpose is to supply an overview and a taste of the large library of works that offer detailed and complex discussions of this topic, both in print and out of print, in India and abroad. Many of these are found in the bibliography, but readers are cautioned that to provide a complete list would not have been feasible, given the sheer volume of materials. Similarly, I have chosen a limited number of performance traditions to discuss; readers should be aware that there are many forms of theater, dance, and music beyond those included here. I have provided a list of films available for students and teachers who wish to utilize them; again, there are many more, but they are often difficult to obtain. The resources of the World Wide Web in this area seem to multiply daily, and as is often the case, are quite uneven in quality and reliability. A good project for students is to try to ferret out some of the truly excellent ones.

I have found in my own teaching that books designed for the introductory level in this area of expertise are very hard to find, and that books written for experts are too technical for my students. They are also often out of print and therefore difficult to obtain for use in college-level classes. It is my hope that students and teachers of the extraordinary performance traditions of India will find this volume useful as a beginning.

I am grateful for all the scholars, across geographical and disciplinary borders, who have devoted their efforts to exploring this topic. If I have misrepresented their work in any way, I am deeply apologetic. I thank the following for their suggestions and observations: Guy Beck, Joyce Burkhalter Flueckiger, Julia M. Hardy, and Da'an Pan. Special thanks are due to those who have contributed and posed for the photographs contained in this volume: Jedediah Baker, photographer; Lizabeth Goldsworthy, photographer; Ramya Ramnarayan, dancer and Director of the Nrithyanjali School of

Dance; Parul Shah, dancer; Shafaatullah Khan, musician; and Phillip Zarrilli. One of the most rewarding moments in a professor's life is when a former student, now poised to become an important scholar, can assist in an academic project. In keeping with long tradition, I gratefully acknowledge the editorial assistance of Lisa W. Crothers. Most of all, I am indebted to India, whose remarkable insight into the nature of performance provides perpetual inspiration.

Transliteration and Romanization

In an effort to make this text accessible to the widest possible readership at an introductory level, I have eliminated all diacriticals, adhering to standard practice in this process. Since the text includes words from Hindi, Sanskrit, and Tamil, as well as words that have become common usage in English, such as mandala, a certain amount of inconsistency would appear in any case. I have adjusted certain names to reflect most common pronunciation, thus Gaṇeśa has become Ganesh. Those who wish to pursue further research on this topic are advised that these diacriticals most often appear as in the examples below. I have listed the most essential terms along with their appearance in this text. Readers should note that the word *rasa* does not possess diacriticals, as opposed to the word rāsa as it appears below: this is discussed at the end of chapter 2. Those unfamiliar with Sanskrit are cautioned that an unfortunate ambivalence regarding the word *Kali* occurs as a result of this process. *Kali,* the designation for the last of the four yugas or ages in Hindu cosmology, looks exactly like *Kālī,* the Goddess, but they are completely different nouns.

ānanda   ananda

Bhadrakāḷi   Bhadrakali

Bhāva   bhava

Bhayānaka	Bhayanaka
Bibhātsa	Bibhatsa
Darśan	Darshan
Dvāpara	Dvapara
Gaṇeśa	Ganesh
Hāsya	Hasya
Holī	Holi
Jagannātha	Jagannatha
Kali, Kālī	Kali
Kaḷarippayaṭṭu	Kalarippayattu
Kālidāsa	Kalidasa
Karuṇa	Karuna
Kathakaḷi	Kathakali
Krishṇa, Kṛṣṇa	Krishna
Kṛishnāṭṭam	Krishnattam
Lakshmī	Lakshmi
Lāsya	Lasya
līlā	lila
Mahābhārata	Mahabharata
māyā	maya
Mohiniyāṭṭam	Mohiniyattam
mokṣa	moksha
Naṭarāja	Nataraja
Nāṭya	Natya
Nāṭyashāstra	Natyashastra
Nṛitta	Nritta
Nṛtya	Nritya
Pārvatī	Parvati

Rādhā	Radha
rāga	raga
rājarasam	rajarasam
Rāmayāṇa	Ramayana
rāsā (rās in Hindi)	raasa, ras
Saraswatī	Saraswati
Saṅgītaratnākara	Sangitaratnakara
Shākuntala	Shakuntala
Shānta	shanta
Shṛṅgāra	shringara
Shūdraka	Shudraka
Tāṇḍava	Tandava
tīrthaṅkara	tirthankara
Tretā	Treta
Vāc	Vac
Vīra	Vira

Rasa

I

A Taste of Things to Come

The performers of music and dance, the transmitters of the religious tradition, speak for Hinduism. We should listen to them.

—Vasudha Narayanan, "Diglossic Hinduism: Liberation and Lentils"

It would be difficult to overstate the significance of performance in Bharat, that ancient civilization now known as India. Performance infuses the culture still, as is apparent from its innumerable forms of music and dance, its active celebration of festivals, and its engagement with images and icons, both on the altars and in the streets. All forms of performance are not created equal in this or any culture, but its centrality in Indian life cannot be challenged. The gift of the Indian for incorporating perform-ance into many aspects of life is a defining quality both in South Asia and in the vast South Asian diaspora. This quality is traditional: a product of millennia of practice; many volumes of textual discussion in philosophi-cal, religious, and artistic quarters; and a long-established methodology of oral transmission. The tradition is perpetually evolving, and provides an arena for lively debate. Changes over time and location, and the influences of traditions from near and far, have always had impact and consequences. In whatever ways the traditions of performance have thus been influ-enced, however, the primacy of performance has remained. Why this should be true particularly in India is one of the questions this volume will endeavor to address.

Our first operating premise is that in some way, performance itself is central to the way the varied cultures within India understand their world, interact with it, and thus produce an active dynamic. The nature of this dynamic may be identified as proceeding from a *religious* sensibility, however diffuse the term "religion" may be. The sources of performative inspiration in India have been religious from the beginning. To what extent they remain so may be a point of contention. The relationship of performance and religion is complex indeed in this context, and one that we will explore in the pages that follow. *Sanatana Dharma*, literally the eternal order and structure of the universe, is the term Hindus sometimes use to designate the ancient religious system that has come to be denoted "Hinduism." The primary sensibility of the oldest texts and the performance traditions was provided by its teachings, but performance in India has never been exclusively Hindu. These aesthetics are shared by Jains, Sikhs, Buddhists, and Parsis as well. Often Indian Christians and Muslims partake of a variety of performance media, and have incorporated a *rasic* sensibility into their own performance traditions. Since Hinduism has not characteristically been a monolithic or an exclusive tradition, the room it has left for wider participation and multiple interpretations has been remarkable.

> Most Indians go to performances of whatever type and experience devotion, wonder, and the like. The experience of devotion, for example, is not confined to . . . devotional performances. The devotional experience arises where it will—it can be in witnessing Lord Krishna's appearance in a village dance-drama, or even in a cinema hall showing a contemporary movie based on Krishna's exploits. (Farley P. Richmond, Darius Swann, and Phillip B. Zarrilli, *Indian Theatre: Traditions of Performance*, 4)

So while Krishna's famous exploits are certainly an aspect of Hindu devotionalism, enactments of them are popular beyond the boundaries of Hinduism.

Bharata, the legendary author of the *Natyashastra*, understood from the outset that there were levels of appreciation. Not everyone is capable of appreciating art at the most elevated standard, but access to the arts is assumed in India, and moreover, it is assumed to offer access to "devotion and wonder." Whether the art form is classical, that is, derived from the formal textual tradition, or a form of folk art, as in the numberless theatrical presentations across South Asia, the potential for religious transformation is inherent in the experience. The distinction between "classical" and "folk" modes of performance is deeply problematic and deceptively oversimplified in India. The boundary between them has probably always been porous. Distinctions may be made in a variety of ways, including the modalities and duration of training, the occasions and location of performance, the identity of the audience, and so forth.[1] Mutual influence between the categories, however, has categorized the relationship. *Rasa,* as a way of describing the design and goals of performance, is an essential part of the vocabulary of performance in most contexts.

Indian aesthetics are extremely complex. It is crucial to remember that in this tradition, the distinction between religion and philosophy that has permeated western culture as well as the western academy is not useful. Both religion and philosophy in India take their inspiration and their application from a worldview that combines them. It is more fruitful to state that the goal of the aestheticians, from Bharatamuni onward, has been to facilitate a transformation—of the artist, the audience, and ultimately the world—that may only be understandable from the perspective of religion. So central has the religious context been to understanding and achieving the goals of performance that it is possible to study the religions of India through her performing arts. The forms performance takes and the ways it is studied, learned, and experienced reveal ways in which *religion* may be understood in India. Further, the study of performance provides a bridge between religion and an even more tenuous term, "spirituality." To push the point further, it is obvious that there is religion *in* the performing arts of India: the ageless mythology, as well as the references to religious paths toward ultimate spiritual goals, have formed the narrative, structural, and teleological goals of music, dance, and drama since ancient times. To consider religion *as* performing arts in India, however, is a different and more complex matter. What does it mean to "perform the divine"? To begin to pursue this, it is necessary to look closely at the Indian approach to aesthetics, and in this way the vital term that titles this study comes into focus.

The fine and performing arts of India are very ancient, though hardly unchanged. Archeological evidence points to dance and music having been an essential feature of South Asian cultures as far back as civilization itself in this part of the world, perhaps even earlier than the second millennium before the Common Era. The oldest texts, the Vedas, Upanishads, and Puranas, include mention of music and dance, as well as provide content for the performing arts. The great epics of the *Ramayana* and the *Mahabharata*, transmitted for long periods by oral tradition before they were committed to written form by the legendary poets Valmiki and Bharata, include descriptions of performance, even as the epics themselves were performed in a wide variety of venues, as they are today. The decisive textual source, the *Natyashastra* attributed to Bharata, is usually dated between the second century before the Common Era (B.C.E.) and the fourth century of the Common Era (C.E.); works predating this monumental work are hard to come by. Thereafter, in an unbroken chain of over fifteen hundred years, the texts proliferated, including commentary on and theoretical discussions of Bharata's treatise as well as additional studies of performance art. The question of accessibility is important: who had the access, and the necessary training, to study such works? In all likelihood, only the *mahagurus*, the holy men and scholars who formed a literate minority, could have possessed such texts, whether in Sanskrit, the classical language of the northern subcontinent, or Tamil, the classical language of the South. India is famous for its many languages and dialects, and texts were likely generated in others of these as well: there was a treasury of textual evidence, much of it lost, much of it still inaccessible in translation. Ultimately, however, the study of texts was not a main component of transmission. To this day, oral tradition remains the primary mode of teaching in the arts of India, as it is in so many other areas of the culture. The written word is sacred, to be sure, but no more so than the spoken word, the chanted or intoned word, and the performed word. Moreover, the subject matter under discussion here often defies language; transmission by example has been much more common. Finally, therefore, although the stated goal of the God Brahma's gift to Bharata of the *Natyashastra* was to offer access to sacred teachings to those other than the Brahmin priesthood, that access has not been by means of the text itself. Rather, the sensibility of the text, along with its guidelines for performance, has been spread throughout the subcontinent by oral transmission and by example in intense and personal contexts.

Accounts regarding the ancient *guru-shishya-parampara* system indicate that the student (*shishya*) lived with the *guru* (teacher) both to serve and to learn the tradition (*parampara*). "*Kula* is the Sanskrit word for family, lineage or house; hence *guru-kula* means learning 'at the house of the guru.'"[2] Sources often maintain that very little talking was done. Rather, the guru would provide, in measured doses, lessons by example, which the student would absorb, copy, and rehearse until the teacher was satisfied. The atmosphere in which teaching and learning took place was oral/aural/kinesthetic. It is difficult to appreciate the power of this form of transmission fully, particularly from the standpoint of a primarily literate culture. If we are to understand the performing arts in India, however, this is one aspect that must be grasped. A distancing occurs between the student and the knowledge to be gained when the mode of transmission is the written word. The physical distance between the eye and the page is symbolic of a greater distance between the learner and the learned. However, when the transmission is experienced physically, as sound enters into the body through the ears and movement is physically internalized, it is more active, more engaged, and it is immediate, that is, unmediated. Those who learn physically learn differently, and experience their knowledge differently as well. It becomes ingested, becomes, like food, part of one's cell structure. When the guru *shows,* rather than *tells,* absorption by the student is of a different quality altogether.

The word *rasa* provides a fascinating study. It is used to describe the primary goals of performing arts in India in all the major literary, philosophical, and aesthetic texts, and provides the cornerstone of the oral traditions of transmission. It is also essential to the study and production of sculpture, architecture, and painting. Interestingly, its primary referent, however, is cuisine. *Rasa* is "taste," "essence," "flavor." How is it possible that a word that can be used to describe a tasty *masala* can also be used to describe a Bharata Natyam performance? Here lies the primary agenda of our effort. The focus will be on how *rasa* defines and informs the traditional performing arts, although reference will be made to its other applications, and finally on how it may be used to describe contemporary and diaspora forms of performance among various Indian communities.

Where taste, sound, image, movement, rhythm, and transformation

meet, therefore, the experience of *rasa* is possible. In India, it has traditionally been the locus of great artistic and spiritual power, where art and
spirit are one. It is to this site in the sacred geography of the Indian imagination that this volume is directed. The term is offered as a lens through
which performance may usefully and creatively be viewed. The fact that
this approach inherently challenges categories and boundaries among religious disciplines and analytical frameworks is one of its more valuable
qualities. *Darshan* describes the visual culture of India, and *mantra* the
oral/aural; *rasa* combines these aspects of the body's experience and adds,
among other factors, the experience of emotional states and their potential to induce religious response. While its origins in ancient times are
clouded and its explication from Bharata onward has often been textual,
rasa as a defining quality of performance has led a full and meaningful life
in the performances of India beyond the textual traditions. In Hindu and
other South Asian settings, while performance *of* text is often a feature of
religious observance, performance *as* text is embraced on many levels as
equally potent. That is, performance contains those qualities perceived in
other religious traditions as present primarily in revealed sacred texts, such
as authority, divine presence, and inspiration, direct and unmediated.
India has many written texts, to be sure, that are understood to possess
transformative qualities. Performances of those texts, or performances
derived from the contents of those texts, are equally powerful. Indeed, a
performance is an essentially creative act, able to initiate and sustain multiple realities as effectively as, and perhaps more immediately than, a written work. Performance thus has special status, not only within but also
beyond the boundaries of religious observance. It is through performative
modes that the sacred becomes palpable in India.

2

Rasa in Theory: Text and Context

For wherever the hand moves, there the glances follow;
Where the glances go, the mind follows;
Where the mind goes, the mood follows;
Where the mood goes, there is the flavour (rasa).

—Nandikeshvara, *Abhinaya Darpana*
  translated by Ananda Coomaraswamy in *The Mirror of Gesture*, 17

ETYMOLOGICAL INGREDIENTS

The Sanskrit word *rasa* (Tamil *irasam*), according to R. S. Khare, may refer "to very sweet fruit juices, as well as to the peppery water which flavors most Tamil meals." *Rasa* can also be "a mixture, concoction, essence of various products."[1] On yet another level it refers to an element that was utilized in Indian alchemy, specifically mercury as a curative agent. The magical qualities of "quicksilver" were believed by alchemists from China to Western Europe to promote physical and spiritual transformation. Mercury is a poison when ingested; the alchemists used it in a variety of ways and were well aware of its deadly qualities. The proper name itself, of course, refers to Greek mythology: Mercury is the Latin for the Greek deity Hermes, the guide of souls and divine messenger. The South Asian equivalent of quicksilver was known as *rajarasam*, the king or lord of drugs, for its many mysterious attributes.[2] Saskia Kersenboom has observed that like the practice of alchemy, "the practice of culture can be seen as an Alchemy of Presence in which the human body forms the central instrument, norm and medium."[3] Nowhere is this more apparent than in the performing arts of India.

As a flavorful "essence," *rasa* is that compilation of essential qualities underlying all food. Food is required not only for the sustenance of the human body but also, in Hindu tradition, as an offering to sustain the divine or macrocosmic body. Most devotional ritual in Indian tradition involves the offering of specially prepared food items, and it is understood that nourishing the divine body is the prerequisite for all life, even as what remains after such ritual offering is then passed among the worshippers as a material expression of a more metaphysical reality. Food must contain the proper balance of *rasa* as flavor (both heating and cooling, sweet and spicy, etc.) in order to promote well-being on both the divine and human levels,[4] and in South Asia, as opposed to other Asian locations and the West, for example, everything must be cooked through—the contributing elements must be fully transformed. Food is understood as fuel, and it must sustain the inner fire of the digestive elements in order for life to continue. Ayurvedic medicine names *rasa* as one of the seven essences that "maintain the integrity of the organism."[5] Briefly, then, all food contains *rasa*; properly prepared food offered to the divine and to the human is a blending and a balance of various forms of *rasa* into a transformed whole. It is then further transformed as the digestive process further "cooks" the food, producing a more refined form of *rasa* that can then nourish the body, contributing variously to the physical constituents of the human form. [6]

Donna M. Wulff selects the following from among the thirty-plus definitions of *rasa* in V. S. Apte's *Sanskrit-English Dictionary*: juice, liquid extract, essence, flavor, and delight. These are meanings that

> are important constituents of its specialized poetic meaning, a relishable "sentiment" or "mood" awakened in the reader or spectator through the combination of elements in a given poem or drama. The standard analogy is that of a blend of a basic food, such as yoghurt, with a number of spices; the resulting substance has a unique flavor (*rasa*) which is not identical with any of the single elements comprising it. *Rasa* is so important to Indian literary critics that it has been termed the soul of poetry, and no criticism of a work of art is considered so devastating as the allegation that it is devoid of *rasa*. ("Religion in a New Mode: The Convergence of the Aesthetic and the Religious in Medieval India," 674)

The crucial elements of *rasa* as they pertain to food are the process of refinement, the balance of qualities, the blend of characteristics, the hidden or underlying basic elements (as stock is to soup), the particular and specific ways in which foods create physical life, and how food produces the transformation of the physical and the metaphysical at once. Rather than thinking of flavoring as an enhancing additive, Indian traditions view flavor as an essential, defining quality of food. One does not add herbs and spices as a separate and intriguing supplement but as part of the process of creation. Indian dishes are named according to the nature of their cooking process and the categories of spices included in that process. Tandoori chicken, for example, is named for the clay oven in which it is cooked and the accompanying spices that give it a particular appearance and taste. Knowing this helps us make sense of the ways in which the term is then applied to the performing arts. In Lee Siegel's words:

> *Rasa* is at once an inner and outer quality as the object of taste, the taste of the object, the capacity of the taster to taste that taste and enjoy it, the enjoyment, the tasting of the taste. The psychophysiological experience of tasting provided a basis for a theory of aesthetic experience which in turn provided a basis for a systemization of a religious experience. (*Sacred and Profane Dimensions of Love in Indian Traditions*, 43)

The senses, taste among them, are acknowledged in Hindu thought as fallible, and responsible in large part for supporting the illusion (*maya*) of the world. In this theory, however, the very senses responsible for the deception may be utilized to surmount it. Far from rejecting the body for its fallibility, Indian aesthetics celebrates its potential to express the transformative ability of its underlying divine nature. Artistic experience *through* the body may enable the attainment of the highest spiritual goals. The relationship of body and mind, spirit and substance, affect and effect are brought together in the Hindu attempt to collapse all of these perceived distinctions, a prerequisite to enlightenment.

Farley P. Richmond has written:

If we equate the theatre experience described in the *Natyashastra* to that of an expert dining on haute cuisine, we may more easily follow the basic aspects of the theory. The spectators are like the connoisseurs of cooked food (called *bhaktas*, literally the "devotees of God") and the performers may be equated both with the chef and the meal. The actors, musicians, dancers, playwrights, and other functionaries are all expected to prepare and train themselves according to the rules and conventions, for the moment when they will offer their lavish feast for the spectators to savor. ("Characteristics of Sanskrit Theatre and Drama," in Richmond, Swann, and Zarrilli, *Indian Theatre: Traditions of Performance*, 81)

A divine and movable feast is offered; the guests are invited to experience, each to his own ability, the alignment of presence and transcendence in the moment of performance. The artists provide access, opportunity, and substance, embodying the potential of the moment quite physically. A particular understanding of divinity is required to approach these lofty goals.

SOURCES OF INSPIRATION

The nature of the divine in Hinduism is understood on many levels. First, as a complex and ancient religious tradition, it possesses the ability to be monotheistic, polytheistic, and henotheistic[7] at once. There is one ultimate divine essence, *Brahman* (monotheism); this essence appears in an endless number of divine forms that may be worshipped and invoked in combination (polytheism); or these may be worshipped one at a time, including several over a single lifetime (henotheism). The eternal, formless, and all-pervading Brahman is capable of generating an infinite number of forms and does so for a variety of purposes, including the manifestation of the world itself. In drama, an actor searches for a character's motivation in order to produce it on stage or film; the actor then "plays" a role. In Hinduism, the motivation underlying this process of infinite manifestation is partly to realize *lila*, divine play.[8] The implications of this are considerable, for it suggests that the divine is inherently "playful," and the term here includes not only a mysterious form of ludic activity but also its inherently dramatic nature. Divine playfulness is not only, or even primarily, a diversionary activity. Rather, it is the means by which the gods create, sustain, and destroy the world. Gods' play is instrumental; it is the origin of all there is. To aspire to participate in lila is to seek to participate in that process. This fact also suggests that Shakespeare's intuition, "all the world's a stage and we but players in it," would have found resonance in South Asia. The concept is known as *maya* in Indian philosophy, and the term is often defined as "illusion." The world as we know it, according to Hindu philosophy, is a dream, a play, an artful construction devised by the divine realm. It is both comedy and tragedy, often simultaneously, and it is ultimately unreal. On the other hand, it is the only reality most humans can know. The divine generates maya by way of lila, providing a variety of paths to true knowledge of what is ultimately real for those who choose to follow them. One of those paths is to study and practice lila, and in so doing, participate in this divine form of creation. The performing arts in India, therefore, offer artists and their audiences this possibility. The end result may include enlightenment, that is, understanding of the ultimate reality, however fleeting. To achieve that goal permanently would be to achieve *moksha*, release from reincarnation, union with Brahman, at once eternal life in bliss and death of the individual ego. Both are reflected in the aesthetic goals of the performing arts.

The Indian understanding of time is another product of Hindu cosmology that has had enormous impact on the design of the performing arts, where it can truly be said that "timing is everything." Time is perceived as circular, an infinite and eternal round of cycles within cycles. The sheer scope of the philosophical exegesis of the nature and duration of time challenges our human ability to absorb it. The four major *yugas*— *krita, treta, dvapara,* and *kali*—take their names from the four throws of the Indian dice game, itself a form of play. They represent declining amounts of *dharma*, righteous or moral behavior and wisdom, in the world. At the beginning of each cycle, the creation is perfect; by its end, *Sanatana Dharma*, eternal and holy order, is gone. At this point, one of the many possible mythological end-time scenarios is engaged, and all returns to a primordial state. The grand total of human years that equals one such cycle, by some calculations, is 4,320,000. But after a period of quiescence, it all begins again. The endless cycles of the macrocosmic calendar echo through all of creation, and every human life is constituted of circuitous patterns that lead repeatedly to death and reincarnation. The only way to break free of this structure is to reach ultimate enlightenment, to understand all this as it truly is: to achieve moksha. But those who may attain it in any given lifetime are few indeed. The performing arts provide one important path toward that goal, in part by emphasizing precisely this circularity inherent in all things. So it is that the dances and the music utilize their own particular languages to underscore circularity. Lewis Rowell has noted that "among the most powerful pressures on the arts of India have been cultural preferences for the circular disposition of space and the cyclical disposition of time," for "temporality in music is understood as a manifestation of the cosmic process of continuous creation" and, of course, of destruction as well.[9] The influence of religious ritual upon the performing arts in ancient times is a major factor, but we may here confront a chicken-and-egg issue: is it a culture's worldview that shapes its ritual or the other way around? Practitioners within a tradition tend not to worry about these kinds of questions; what is really important is that the themes of primary significance be consistently affirmed and their content probed for meaning. This is certainly the case where the circular theory of time is concerned in India. India has consistently looked to her performing arts for this affirmation, and she has not been disappointed.

A WRITTEN RECIPE FOR THE ARTS

Aesthetic theory in India certainly predates the *Natyashastra*, but this text is the earliest extant document that we have. It is part theatrical manual, part philosophy of aesthetics, part mythological history, part theology. Its goals include providing a precise description of stage construction and equally precise guidelines for the movements, facial expressions, and *mudras* (often used synonymously with the term *hastas*) or hand gestures to be used in performance. All of these are contextualized in a larger understanding of the goals of performance, the nature of the performance space, and performers. For Bharata, who committed these guidelines to the written word, the dramatic arts included the categories of what we would recognize as drama/the-ater, poetry, dance, and music. Beyond these, his guidelines apply to representation of these arts in sculpture, and the location and creation of these arts in architecture, both as performance and as architectural enhancement on friezes and iconography. In short, the *Natyashastra* is an exhaustive, encyclopedic dissertation on the arts, with an emphasis on performing arts as its central feature. It is also full of invocations to deities, acknowledging the divine origins of the arts and the central role performance plays in achieving divine goals. It is clear that in Bharata's text, and in the tradition that uses it as a primary resource, *rasa* and those arts that attempt to achieve it hold transcendence of the microcosmic reality as their ultimate purpose. The story of the text's origins leaves no question as to its divine source, Brahma, and it is often called the Fifth Veda.

For Bharata, and the many commentators and aestheticians who followed him, the issues of performance, therefore, were not primarily issues of entertainment as it is normally understood today. It was rather a matter of how performance might be the means to a very different experience. The components of performance art were precisely defined and structured, not to inhibit creativity but to enable it. Individual creativity and self-expression were irrelevant: divine creativity and the expression of ultimate reality were the goals. Today, when we study these texts on aesthetics, our tendency is to marvel at the strict guidelines for dancers, poets, dramatists, musicians, architects, and sculptors, and wonder how creativity could flourish under such precise formulations. But we are using the wrong paradigms altogether. Moreover, one might argue that these artists, working within these parameters, had to develop an extremely subtle form of creativity. In truth, Indian arts allow for enormous innovation, but it often must exist "between the lines," and may only be recognized by those trained to discern it. It could be argued that *rasa* can only occur when an artist is mature and expert enough to create within the interstices of the rules.

The first book of the *Natyashastra* describes the origins of drama and attributes both the activity and the contents of the text to the creator deity Brahma. The practice of the dramatic arts is praised as a comprehensive aid to the learning of virtue, proper behavior, ethical and moral fortitude, courage, love, and adoration of the divine realm. The enjoyment and pleasure that result from such practices are encouraged as conducive to an appreciation of all the branches of learning. By the end of the *Natyashastra* its contents are praised as promoting worldly and otherworldly goals as significant as those attained by the practice of formal religious ritual. Like the elaborate rituals described in the Vedic texts, the theater offers in microcosm a representation of the greater, macrocosmic realities, and in so doing, allows those prepared to understand a path to transcendence. Later commentaries develop this theme in increasingly abstract and often esoteric terms.

The great contemporary Indian scholar and commentator Kapila Vatsyayan has written that the worldview of the *Natyashastra* is organic and dynamic. It proceeds through paradox: impersonality and intensity;[10] the specific and the universal; the inner and the outer; the *bindu* (point) and its projection into infinite variety; stillness and movement; the physical body and its transcendence; the crucial nature of form, its development into a multitude of forms, and its final movement beyond form. "The artistic experience is acausal and whole, a state of beatitude and bliss in the mind of the experiencer, the creator."[11] *Rasa* is "the highly charged state of momentary freedom and emancipation which motivates, inspires creation . . . [and] this experience . . . facilitates an abstraction of life into its primary emotions and sentiments."[12] When the *Natyashastra* provides explicit instructions for the performance area as "sacralized cosmic space," the author is "consecrating space which would prepare actors, performers and audience to be transported to the world of the imagination and simultaneously to the divine and heavenly."[13] When he describes the location of the drama in time, he simultaneously describes "physical duration" and "a conceptual time where gods and humans meet." He views "the goal of artistic creation as a tool to evoke a *rasa* . . . and not to look at or imitate actuality," for "the search for 'totality' and 'wholeness' . . . is primary." To achieve this goal, "eschewing of the particular 'I' is a primary demand."[14] The result is "sensual and spiritual at once."[15] These qualities make "the work of art have the potential to rise above pain and pleasure, desire or suffering. The artistic work embodies and, in turn, stimulates, a state of awareness and consciousness which is akin to the experience of Brahman."[16] Because it is fleeting, this state is not identical with the final and ultimate goal of spiritual discipline; it is, however, a momentary glimpse of that transformative achievement.

Book 6, lines 42–45 of the *Natyashastra* describes eight *rasas*, and iden-
tifies them as associated with both colors and deities. The details and characteristics of Bharata's scheme of classification have continued to influence
performance traditions over the centuries.

Rasa	Color	Deity
shringara (love in union and separation)	*shyama* (green)	Vishnu
hasya (humor)	*sita* (white)	Pramatha
karuna (pathos, sorrow)	*kapota* (dove-colored)	Yama
raudra (anger, wrath)	*rakta* (red)	Rudra (later Shiva)
vira (heroism)	*gaura* (wheat brown)	Mahendra
bhayanaka (fear/panic)	*krishna* (black)	Kala
bibhatsa (distaste/recoil/disgust)	*nila* (blue)	Mahakala
abdhuta (wonderment/surprise)	*pita* (yellow)	Brahma

A ninth *rasa, shanta*, normally defined as peace/tranquility/enlightened
repose, was added in the eighth century of the Common Era and has been
accepted as an essential component of the schema. These *rasas* are
described as consisting of precise performative postures, characteristic
qualities of movement, facial expressions, and mudras or hand gestures.

Several aspects of this system are notable. First, each *rasa* response may
be generated by a number of different emotive stimuli (or determinants):
the *bhavas*, the particular and basic emotions or moods. *Rasa* "has the
same relation to the bhava as wine has to the grapes, sugar and herbs
which compose it and which dissolve and blend completely in an intoxi-
cant of entirely different character."[17] For example, the *rasa hasya* (humor)
may be a result of impudence, physical exaggeration or clowning, or
laughter at oneself or at others. *Karuna* (pathos) may result from separation, death, physical impediment, and so forth. According to the text,
there are forty-nine bhavas that interact to influence *rasa* response, and
one cannot exist without the other: "There is no *Rasa* devoid of *Bhava* nor
Bhava devoid of *Rasa*."[18] And although the *rasas* may be understood as
sentiments, they are *never* achieved by sentimentality. They may appear to

result from emotion, but to be emotional is to lose any possibility of attaining the goal. One *must* distinguish between any personal ego-oriented function and the actual, transpersonal, transcendent purpose. To fail is to embrace mediocrity, to be seduced and entrapped by maya.

It is also notable that although exact dating of the text is problematic, certain details remind us that the tradition has been constantly evolving, for here, Shiva is not named, but his earlier and less imposing persona, Rudra ("the howler"), is featured. This may indicate a location of the text in time or a perspective born of geographical location, for different deities have been worshipped differently in the diverse cultures of South Asia over time. Similarly, although "*krishna*" is used as a color designation, there is no mention of Krishna as deity. Most likely both chronology and location are involved. The deities highlighted as associated with the *rasas* are Vedic, and the text hearkens to the Vedic corpus frequently. This fact confirms the Sanskritic/North Indian origins of the *Natyashastra*. But the text permeated the subcontinent thoroughly, and has been applied to performing arts north and south.

The fact that Bharata indicates colors in association with these emotive archetypes is not surprising in South Asia, where even the caste system is called *varna*, a system of color designation. Indians are extremely sensitive to color, as are most cultures born of tropical and subtropical climates. The richness of the color palette is one of the defining qualities of Indian life. Traditional performing arts utilize guidelines for color to express emotive states in costuming and make-up, as visual cues, to this day. Bharata's guidelines are like a menu from which the flavors may be used in endless combination to produce the requisite balance of aesthetic tastes. These cues are internalized by performers and audiences alike within South Asian cultures from an early age, and response becomes instinctive.

INFLUENCES AND IMPLICATIONS

Just as a rich flavor leaves an aftertaste and a flash of light and color leaves an afterimage in our perception, the *Natyashastra* was followed by many centuries of commentary and development. The effect was a deepening and expansion of Bharata's treatise. By the tenth or eleventh century of the Common Era, one of the greatest commentators on the *Natyashastra*, Abhinavagupta, appeared. For this aesthetician, "the aesthetic experience is *ananda* . . . it is self-luminous and self-conscious, devoid of all duality and multiplicity."[19] A Kashmiri Shaivite philosopher, he theorized that "in art the purified state of undifferentiated experience was *rasa* or *ananda*."[20] Thus *rasa* becomes "a state of consciousness"[21] akin to the bliss (ananda) of the enlightened, liberated soul. Study of the corpus of the primary text and its centuries of commentary have led Kapila Vatsyayan to state that Indian art is not "religious in the ordinary sense, nor is there a theology of aesthetics, but the two fields interpenetrate because they share the basic world-view in general and the specific goal of *moksha* and liberation in particular."[22]

For Abhinavagupta, the term *rasa* "is of central importance for interpreting religious experience."[23] "Situations portrayed in drama or poetry are shorn of their particularity. . . . Abhinava speaks of *rasa* as transcending the time and space of both the original character and the actor." "One transcends all desires and limited, ego-bound perceptions,"[24] fulfilling the aspiration of all the major spiritual disciplines of India whose goal is *moksha*. Writing about poetry, but clearly referring to the aesthetic goal in general, Abhinava asserts:

> Once a *rasa* has been thus realized, its enjoyment (is possible), an enjoyment which is different from the apprehensions derived from memory or direct experience and which takes the form of melting, expansion, and radiance. This enjoyment is like the bliss that comes from realizing (one's identity) with the highest Brahman, for it consists of repose in the bliss which is the true nature of one's own self. (*Locana*, 2.4, in Ingalls, Masson, and Patwardhan, *The Dhvanyaloka of Anandavardhana with the Locana of Abhinavagupta*, 222)

Theories regarding Sanskrit poetics parallel, and reflect their kinship with, the dramatic arts consistently over time. Book 17 of the *Natyashastra* is wholly devoted to the characteristics of poetry, for the spoken word was central to traditional theater. To the same extent as movement and music, the poetry of performance was understood as essential in creating and supporting the goals of the dramatic arts. Sushil K. De has observed that the

> blissful condition reproduced . . . by the idealized creation of poetry is given as almost equivalent to the philosophical *ananda*. In explaining that it affords an escape from the natural world by replacing it with an imaginative world, Sanskrit theorists rightly emphasize that, even from the reader's point of view, the function of art is that of the deliverer. (*Sanskrit Poetics as a Study of Aesthetic*, 69)

Poetry in recitation, as it was used in Sanskrit dramatic performance and is still used to this day across India in constantly evolving traditions of live performance, shares with written poetry the potential to provide the experience of *rasa*. That is, it offers the potential for transformation.

The continuing tradition of further explication is exemplified by the publication of a text entitled the *Abhinaya Darpana of Nandikeshvara* in 1874. Ananda Coomaraswamy (1877–1947), the renowned art historian, whose extensive, extraordinary, and scholarly opus is an invaluable resource, translated the work into English as *The Mirror of Gesture*. In his introduction to this text, he observes:

> The arts are not for our instruction, but for our delight, and this delight is something more than pleasure, it is the godlike ecstasy of liberation from the restless activity of the mind and the senses, which are the veils of all reality, transparent only when we are at peace with ourselves. (*The Mirror of Gesture*, 9)

This relatively small treatise is an encyclopedia of gesture. Coomaraswamy included in his translation examples of the gestures described therein by providing plates from ancient sculpture and statuary, as well as portrayals by a human in photographs. The evidence is clear, as are the implications: this language of gesture has existed in the performing arts as well as in the static arts in India, each mirroring the other, each reinforcing and supporting the other, for millennia. The concept of *rasa* has provided the paradigm, the purpose, and the performative premise throughout a process of evolution that has characterized both the performing arts and the commentaries on them.

One major source of influence whose importance cannot be overstated is the religious movement identified as *Bhakti*. While the term appears in the Vedic sources, often in reference to devotional poetry, Bhakti as a religious movement seems to have flowered first in Tamil Nadu in the far south of the subcontinent, during the seventh to ninth centuries.[25] It spread throughout much of the subcontinent in medieval India. And while the term is often translated simply as a category of activity performed in devotion to a deity, most often Krishna or Shiva, its implications for religious life are more complex than that definition suggests. This form of devotion requires an active engagement in service of a deity, often with elements of mythology associated with that deity: that is, an enactment, a performance, a celebration, including music and dance. Out of the love and longing associated with shringara *rasa*, a new *rasa* was generated by devotees, namely, bhakti *rasa*. It shares with the *rasa*s enumerated by Bharata its genesis in bhava, emotion; the challenge is to use that emotion to achieve an impersonal state of heightened awareness, building toward the ultimate goal of transformation. The means to this end are, however, quite different from the sort of performance Bharata had in mind. These songs and dances are performed by amateurs, in nontheatrical venues, and therefore in much less formal and structured contexts.

In the Bengali Vaishnava cult as described by David Kinsley, devotees celebrate the mythology of Krishna according to their own particular understanding of which bhavas are appropriate to the story and will provide the most intimate encounter with the deity. Relationships the deity had during his incarnation in this world are highlighted, especially the love affair between Krishna and the woman Radha, immortalized in the poetry of the *Gita Govinda* and other texts, both written and oral. The participant seeks to achieve the transpersonal state that *rasa* implies.

He is required, as is the aesthetic connoisseur, to lose himself in the mood of the drama, to resist involving his own personal desires and emotions. Before he can soar to the heights of all-consuming love for Krishna he must forget himself, disassociate himself from those particular circumstances and feelings that make him unique.[26]

Some of the methodologies known from acting are utilized to assist participants in achieving this goal. In practice, these performances are noted for their ability to inspire ecstatic fervor. As is true in the more classical traditions, then, bhakti *rasa* provides a bodily experience of a transcendent reality. But the context is entirely different.

From the etymological point of view, it is fascinating (and perhaps confusing!) to note that another Sanskrit term, *raasa* (*raas* in Hindi), is used to identify the singing and especially the circle dancing performed in devotion to Krishna, as well as Shiva. *Raas lila*, the play/performance associated with ecstatic worship of these deities, is a well-known component of religious practice during festivals throughout India; "raas" is often used more generally to refer to a variety of circular dances. "*Rasa*" and "raasa" are completely different words that refer to different forms of expressive action. But certainly they share the larger sensibility that pervades performance in the complex of cultures that have informed India's traditions. Performance, in both cases, offers the possibility of presence and transcendence, a path through bodily experience toward ultimate and religiously defined transformation, whether that is understood as ecstatic worldly union with a deity (raasa) or a taste (rasa) of liberation from the maya of existence.

3

Rasa in Practice: Drama, Dance, Music

The following sections will describe essential aspects of drama, dance, and music as they pertain to the theme of rasa. These descriptions are necessarily limited in scope, and the reader is encouraged to seek out more detailed examinations of these and other artistic forms.

ALL THE STAGE IS BUT A WORLD . . .

The Sanskrit play begins with a short ceremony in which the director and his Assistant, or an actress, celebrate their magical function of turning pretense into reality. (Edwin Gerow in Barbara Stoler Miller, *The Plays of Kalidasa, Theater of Memory*, 45)

In Bharata's terminology, the bare text of a drama is called "poetry" . . . while the Text arranged for performance is called "drama." . . . In later critical literature, drama is called "visual poetry" . . . as opposed to "aural poetry" because it presents us with a world to see. (Miller, *The Plays of Kalidasa*, 17)

It could be argued that every stage performance seeks to create a world. The nature of that world is culturally defined, that is, it is a product of cultural variables. The variables in this creative process are many, and include geography, chronology, history, political and sociological influences, and, particularly in South Asia, religious sensibility. Because theatrical traditions in India are so ancient and complex, the worlds created by the Sanskrit dramatists based on the writings of Bharata may be difficult to imagine; the fact that these dramas are largely lost adds to the conundrum. There are survivors, however, plays and poetry that can help guide the serious student in an exploration of this milieu. To begin, it is necessary to understand that when the ancient dramatists created their works, their concerns were quite different from those of current artists in either India or the West.

> Many forms of Indian performance do not fit neatly into Western categories. Music and bodily movement are requisite parts of any performance. The individual performer in an ensemble may be a specialist in music or acting-dance, but each specialist also must have an intimate knowledge of the other arts necessary for the successful performance. Actor-dancers will be required to possess as part of their embodied performance knowledge of the rhythmic patterns of the music to which they must perform. Instrumentalists or vocalists will just as assuredly be immersed in the patterns of movement, stage conventions, and methods of character creation used by the actor-dancers. (Farley P. Richmond, Darius Swann, and Phillip B. Zarrilli, *Indian Theatre: Traditions of Performance*, 5)

According to Bharata, the performing arts were integrated to an extraordinary degree in Indian traditions. This is still apparent in most performing arts on the subcontinent. The categories that make the most sense are those that distinguish the aesthetic goals of a performance, rather than attempt to classify whether that performance is composed primarily of drama, dance, or music. The design of a theater in ancient India "was considered a branch of temple architecture." "After all, the *Natyashastra* describes the performance of a play as a sacrifice to the gods."[1] In all likelihood, plays were performed in structures attached to temples, and the audience was probably understood to include the divine host. "The numerous rituals accompanying the building of the theatre, the stages in its construction, its consecration, and the preliminaries preceding the performance of a play strengthen the contention that dramatic events were thought of as sacred affairs."[2]

The actual contents of such plays varied widely, and it would be a mistake to assume that they were purely devotional. Although Sanskrit drama is largely lost to us, the texts that remain suggest a wide variety of topics were addressed. *Shakuntala,* written by Kalidasa in the fifth century of the Common Era, and *The Little Clay Cart,* ascribed to King Shudraka, possibly from the fourth century of the Common Era, are two examples that have survived and been embraced not only in India but also on the world stage; there are also extant plays by Bhasa, Bhavabhuti, and others. The two examples cited above feature courtly romance, human struggle, and considerable insight into the cultural milieu that gave them form and content. While the presentations of these works were surrounded by ritual and the architecture of the theater itself was specifically based on principles derived from religious practice, the dramas are concerned with the overcoming of human weakness by human strength and insight.

While Sanskrit dramas contain references to and characterizations of religious belief and religious figures, their focus is much more on this world than on a divine realm. This fact, however, does not make them secular. That is, religious sensibility does not require a religious subject, by the western definition of those terms. There need not be explicit mention of deities, beliefs, or practices for a spiritual concern to be present. In a culture where the macrocosmic (divine reality) and microcosmic (human or worldly reality) spheres so often overlap, and both operate within the dream of maya, those sorts of distinctions are much more difficult to discern. Moreover, the ultimate goal of *rasa* becomes accessible, as described by Bharata, through the experience of emotion, first as bhava, the common and specific form aroused by connection through sympathy grounded in personal experience. If that emotional intensity is generated and processed as required, the refinement that leads to *rasa* is the result. The best analogy, again, is to the cooking process. When properly prepared and measured ingredients are added in the correct order and quantity, heated at precisely the correct temperature for exactly the correct duration, a transformation visibly and tastefully occurs. The final result is a refined product.

To enable the process, characterization and attention to form were considered foremost. "Richly painted scenery and ornate sets were alien to Hindu taste. Descriptive poetry effectively took the place of painted scenery or heavy sets, which tend to dwarf the personality of the actor."[3] For the performer, acting was "considered a discipline (*yoga*) whereby the actor and acted become one."[4] The use of the word "*yoga*" in this context is crucial. It reminds us that the goal of the performance transcends any sort of personal realization or gratification. "The elements interact to produce the play's emotional integration or *rasa*, which, as formulated by the theoretical tradition, is a resolution of sentiments sufficiently general to abolish the mundane distinctions between audience, actor, and author."[5] The content and plot of such plays were also designed to fulfill purposes beyond their deceptively courtly context. Questions are raised and conflicts abound, but Sanskrit theater seeks the resolution of its tension within the body of the work. Whatever twists and turns the plot and characters might take, by the end of the piece balance is restored on every level, and worldly dharma is affirmed. The characters interact with the natural world as aspects of it: there is no sense of "man against nature," as one often finds in theater of the West.[6] And "the patterns of the Indian dramatic universe move toward a closure" in which the various elements combine to produce "an environment of auspicious relations expressive of cosmic renewal."[7]

As was also the case with dance and music, as we shall see, the time of day at which any drama was staged was determined by its *rasic* orientation.

> The subject matter of the play determined the time of the performance. A play based on a tale of virtue was performed before noon; a play rich in instrumental music, unfolding a story of strength and energy, in the afternoon; a play of erotic sentiments in the first part of the night; and plays of pathetic sentiments in the fourth part of the night. No plays were presented at midnight, at midday or at the time of evening prayers. Mostly, dramatic performances were held in the afternoon and lasted four or five hours. (Balwant Gargi, *Theatre in India*, 13)

Plays were performed to mark any number of special occasions, many connected with the royal courts. The rajas or kings of ancient India were usually considered to have divine attributes and semidivine identity; their ambiguous nature effectively blurs the line between the macrocosm and the microcosm. To highlight this theme of ambivalence, Kalidasa's plays target the abiding tension between the demands of dharma and the pull of worldly desire. This tension defines human life and is itself a reflection of the larger divine tension in Hindu cosmology. Resolution restores harmony on both levels, in part by stripping away the illusion of the apparent discontinuity or conflict between macrocosm and microcosm, duty and passion. The goal of a Sanskrit drama is to reestablish emotional harmony in the microcosm of the audience by exploring the deeper relations that bind apparent conflicts of existence. The manifestation of these relations produces the intense aesthetic experience called *rasa*.[8]

The success of any given performance was to be measured, according to Bharata, on many levels. Proper response on the part of the audience to the genesis of emotional reaction, in human terms, would be vocal and facial, that is, all the sorts of feedback one would expect. For the Sanskrit dramatist, however, just as there is a higher level of performance, there is a higher level of reception of that performance.

> The attainment of the highest degree of excellence in performance, however, is regarded from the perspective of the gods. When the response is not a tumultuous commotion, when there is in fact not the slightest sound or disturbance among the audience, even in a packed house—that success is regarded as divine. (David Gitomer in Miller, *The Plays of Kalidasa,* 81)

That higher level of attainment is the experience of *rasa*.

DANCE AS MYSTERY

O body swayed to music, O brightening glance,
How can we know the dancer from the dance?

—William Butler Yeats, "Among School Children"

The word "mystery" comes to us from ancient Greece, where it signified a particular collection of rituals associated with the cult at Eleusis.

In its original context, *mysterion* was a form of practice inaccessible to the uninitiated. The first sense of the word, then, was a reference to religious performance. It is not difficult to imagine how it came to suggest insoluble puzzles with dark associations: such ritual was "mysterious" because no one would speak of it outside the cult. It occurred largely at night, often in caves, and it involved symbolic and actual experiences of a transforming nature, having to do with death and rebirth—Eleusis was the site of the cult of the goddess Demeter. There are many words in Indian languages to describe the dance event, but "mystery" captures much of the essence, once we know the etymology. For the temple dances of South Asia were, in fact, ritual events, designed to effect transformation, dedicated to divine forces, embodying creative energies having to do with fertility, regeneration, and the cycles of birth and death. The ritual specialists were performers of consummate skill who led lives circumscribed by the temples. And while the performance might be accessible to a variety of audiences depending upon the occasion and the rules of the particular group, the "true" audience was those both prepared for and inclined to understand its highest aesthetic goals, the *rasikas*, or enlightened observers. A divine audience was often believed to be present as well.

Beyond the temples, in the courts and in the larger culture generally, dance has always been at the center of Hindu life. The festivals and ceremonies that are celebrated all over the subcontinent feature dance as a matter of course, whether it is one of the infinite variety of folk dances, carefully choreographed or simply general popular knowledge; a dancing parade to celebrate a deity or a mythological story; or the welcoming of the bridegroom by his future wife's family for his wedding, which also includes circumambulation of the sacred fire. This ritual is probably as ancient as Hinduism itself, and may have been the starting point for the many circling dances that are still prominent in village India. Shanta Serbjeet Singh has written that dance is "the ultimate metaphor" of India's worldview, that is, "it holds up the clearest mirror to the Indian vision of life on earth."[9] The most visible indication that India has always taken dance seriously is the fact that so many of the deities in the Hindu pantheon are dancers: Shiva, Parvati, Ganesh, Krishna, Kali . . . the list is too long to include all of them.

FIGURE 3.1 The Goddess Parvati, spouse of Shiva, is both dancer and musician. In this image she takes the traditional *tribhangi* or *tribhanga* posture familiar in both iconography and dance, as the legs, torso, and head angle in three contrary directions. LIZABETH GOLDSWORTHY

FIGURE 3.2 Lord Ganesh, destroyer of obstacles, lord of transitions, is a patron of the arts as well as a performer. LIZABETH GOLDSWORTHY

FIGURE 3.3 Krishna as a child dances on the multiple heads of the defeated serpent king, Kaliya. LIZABETH GOLDSWORTHY

FIGURE 3.4 Krishna as a young man is famous for his dances with the cowherding *gopis*. LIZABETH GOLDSWORTHY

This may seem an extraordinary theological premise from the perspective of other cultures where dance has often been looked upon with suspicion by religious institutions, but in South Asia it is perfectly natural. The sheer quantity of dance forms and dancers in the culture to this day, the obvious use of dance in the many festivals that populate the religious calendar, as well as folk dances beyond number are consistent with an inherent expectation that dance not only will occur but also is prized, honored, and designated as a divinely inspired activity. Where the gods and goddesses are dancers, the humans are sure to be dancers as well. Heinrich Zimmer wrote:

> Dancing is an ancient form of magic. The dancer becomes amplified into a being endowed with supra-normal powers. His personality is transformed. Like yoga, the dance induces trance, ecstasy, the experience of the divine, the realization of one's own secret nature, and, finally, mergence into the divine essence. In India the dance has flourished side by side with the terrific austerities of the meditation grove—fasting, breathing exercises, absolute introversion. To work magic, to put enchantment upon others, one has first to put enchantments on oneself. And this is effected as well by the dance as by prayer, fasting and meditation. Shiva, therefore, the arch-yogi of the gods, is necessarily also the master of the dance. (*Myths and Symbols in Indian Art and Civilization*, 151)

As Zimmer observed, it is true that those who dance often experience an ecstasy that is both physical and psychological. In India, however, there is still more involved. Dance is a creative act in an ultimate sense of the term. *Shiva Nataraja*, literally Shiva as Lord of the Dance, actually dances the universe into being, and then destroys it in the same way. The physical contact of the foot against the ground is sacred, for it precipitates existence. What is lifeless and dormant is animated by the touch of the foot; hence the soles of the dancers' feet are painted red, the auspicious color associated with growth and fertility. Hindu iconography pays considerable attention to the feet, for although they are the lowest part of the body, and thus in several ways the least elevated, they also connect the body to the sacred earth. When a shishya or student touches her guru's feet in humility and thanks, therefore, the act is meaningful on several levels. Almost all Indian dancers wear ankle bells; for a beginner, one of the ceremonies that marks her entrance into the dance world is the ritual presentation of these essential accessories. The bells emphasize the intricate footwork with which the dancer enacts his or her relationship both with the divine dancers and with the sacred ground, as well as the rhythm that is central to the performance.

The mythological exegesis of Shiva's dance is extensive and varied, from the Sanskrit Puranas to the textual and iconographic representations associated with Chidambaram, the South Indian center of his worship in his form as Nataraja. Stella Kramrisch has written that Nataraja's dance is "the expression of his divine totality. His dancing limbs convey by their movements and symbols the fivefold action of creation, maintenance, dissolution, veiling-unveiling, and liberation."[10] In most versions of the story, Shiva initially dances to subdue an arrogant assemblage of demons and/or sages who have attempted to assert their superiority, a familiar theme in Hindu mythology. It is shown that this dance underlies all of existence, and its demise.

Shiva's *tandava* dance is a fierce and violent manifestation, both wild and controlled, creative and destructive. His *lasya* dance balances it with gentle lyricism. The iconographical representation of Shiva Nataraja is one of the most recognizable of India's many images of the divine. His hair flies out behind and to the sides of his face, where often the long coils are attached to a bronze icon loosely, so that they move. But his face is impassive, distant. The icon is both dynamic and still. He holds the drum in one hand, for the rhythm of the dance is the heartbeat of the world, its sound the seed of all that is. In another hand he holds a flame, and he dances in a ring of flame. Fire is the energy that both produces and destroys life, a particularly potent image in a culture that cremates the dead. It also gives light, which hearkens to the light of wisdom, as in "enlightenment." Shiva dances on the body of the dwarf or demon, Apasmara Purusha, who represents ignorance. Shiva Nataraja is one of the richest images on the subcontinent; a thorough exegesis would easily fill a volume itself.

The seven most commonly acknowledged dances of the classical repertoire of South Asia are Bharata Natyam, Odissi, Kathak, Kathakali,

FIGURE 3.5 Shiva Nataraja in a classic representation of his *tandava* dance.
LIZABETH GOLDSWORTHY

Kuchipudi, Manipuri, and Mohiniyattam. The classical distinction accorded to these specific forms is an indication that they were traditionally attached to the temples, although they often also had formal affiliations to the great courts of the rajas, the kings, of the many kingdoms that made up South Asia until modern times (many existed until independence in 1947). As Shovana Narayan observes, "in the Indian context the term 'classical' also denotes adhering to the principles of the 'shastras' (treatises on the codification of the various arts); in other words, there is an inherent spirit of Sanskritization."[11] But all of these dance forms interpreted and embodied the classical tradition in ways strongly influenced by geography, history, and the diverse preferences for movement associated with ethnic group identities.

After the arrival of Islam in the eighth century of the Common Era, the Moghul courts that spread across much of northern India continued to support performers. In some cases South Asian Islam constrained traditional performance modes, for Islamic theology could not support the Hindu premises upon which the dances had been based. The resulting influence on the arts was considerable, but it must also be observed that in many cases a flowering of artistic creativity characterized the meeting of West and South Asian traditions. The dancers themselves came from hereditary communities that once flourished with talented musicians, dancers, costume artists, make-up artists—in short, all the supporting craftspeople without whom the performers could not function. They lived remarkable lives unique in South Asia, for while they may not have been born into a high caste, they were acknowledged for their artistry and had a measure of independence as well as material well-being. Women performers were often educated and literate, knowledgeable beyond the arts.

The aesthetics of dance are typically detailed. Some of the many distinctions used to describe the range of performance types are these:

NRITTA: pure, abstract, or decorative dance

NRITYA: mimetic dance, dominated by gestures that correspond to the narrative or theme of the performance

NATYA: dance with a high content of dramatic acting, using specific body gestures outlined in the tradition

TANDAVA: movements associated with the masculine gender, typically
vigorous, strenuous, strong
LASYA: movements associated with the feminine gender, typically fluid,
graceful and lyrical

—(Richmond, Swann, and Zarrilli, *Indian Theatre*, 5)

It is vital to remember that all of these types are normally integrated into a
performance. And both male and female dancers use the gendered movements. Often, for example, a female dancer will portray both Krishna and
his human consort, Radha, in the same piece. There are many signals for a
change in character that are normative, but obviously the change in the
type of movement is key. In dance forms that were traditionally restricted
by gender, like Kathakali and Kuchipudi, a form from Andhra Pradesh,
male dancers would regularly portray females. To see such a performance
is really illuminating. When a male dancer "becomes" female, something
else altogether is created, almost as if a third gender has come into being.
This crossing of gender lines is totally in keeping with the nature of the
divine in Hinduism, as portrayed in the iconography of *Shiva Ardha-
narishvara*, in which the great lord is portrayed as both male and female,
divided vertically. What happens when the genders are combined is more
than the sum of its parts, and more than biology can explain.

The dancer of any classical Indian form learns a vocabulary of postures
that convey meaning. She or he is a *mandala*, in the traditional Indian
sense of the word, dynamically turning on her or his own axis. In its
graphic form, utilized by Hindus and Buddhists across Asia, a mandala is
a two-dimensional representation of a three-dimensional reality, used in
rituals from the simple to the complex to sacralize space in a variety of
ways, but always to concentrate spiritual energies and provide a focus for
meditation or other sacred acts. It supplies a map, a spatial orientation, a
physical blueprint for a journey toward a transcendent reality. Temples in
Hindu tradition are three-dimensional mandalas serving the same function. In dance, the mandala takes on the third dimension of depth in the
body of the performer, and adds presence and movement. The dancer is a
living embodiment of a sacred map that displays a path to enlightenment.

Just as the galaxies of the manifest world spun around their own axis, so did the body as *mandala*. . . . So was the dance conceived of as a series of patterns in which the body, as the link between the earth and the heavens, became an analogue to the unmanifest world. (Shanta Serbjeet Singh, *Indian Dance: The Ultimate Metaphor,* 12)

Abhinaya is the proper name for the use of the elements of gesture in performance to produce a predetermined effect. It is part mime, part sign language, part choreography: the embodiment of a language. Its function is, on the one hand, to produce a quality of performance on the part of the actor, and on the other hand, to produce a quality of response on the part of the observer. From the *Natyashastra* onward in the philosophical tradition, explication of this vocabulary of expression, including both posture and gesture, is understood as exploring the most profound premises of performance and religion. That is, the elements are combined to produce *rasa*.

Bharata Natyam

Of the many art forms that have ancient roots in South Asia, Bharata Natyam is one that has captured the imagination of the international performing arts community in remarkable fashion, and its success makes for a fascinating tale. It has come to symbolize the continuity of tradition and its value to new generations, separated in space and time, and often cultural context, from India. For continuity to exist, commitment must be strong and palpable, and there is plentiful evidence that such has been the case. An *Arangetram* marks the occasion when a young dancer literally "takes the stage," or the performance space, for the first time before her audience. Bharata Natyam has itself taken the stage in the past century. Among the dance communities in India, the evolution of this form is a fairly controversial topic, characterized by some very radical changes. Anne-Marie Gaston, in her detailed study *Bharata Natyam: From Temple to Theatre,* has charted this transformation in depth. It is clear that *natya* was an ancient form of worship in South Asia, and that dancers were considered crucial in South Indian temples and elsewhere on the subcontinent as far back as textual and archeological evidence allow us to determine. However, a specific dance called "Bharata Natyam" did not exist until the 1930s, when it was produced largely under the influence of Rukmini Devi and others of her generation determined to rescue classical temple dancing from oblivion. Devi studied the dance form traditional in Tamil Nadu, called *dasi attam*, and set out to reform and preserve it.

An assortment of associations with the dance were problematic during the twentieth century; not least was its history of association with the dedication of young women to temples, outlawed in 1947. The British occupation of South Asia had dramatic impact on all the arts, of course, and this negative influence is still a factor in how the arts are understood and transmitted among Indian communities worldwide. Rukmini Devi and those with whom she worked endeavored to rescue classical temple dancing by presenting it in such a way that it could survive in a new India as an acknowledged form of performance art. Others have argued persuasively that what appears on proscenium stages under the banner of Bharata Natyam bears little resemblance to the traditional temple dances, that it has become gentrified, sanitized, and that the very efforts that created this form conspired with the forces of history and intolerance to obliterate the genuine artistic heritage.

What the written sources and historical evidence tell us is that dancing was sacred, and was, in fact, a means to accessing the highest levels of understanding described by Indian philosophical and religious texts. It was performed for the refinement and enlightenment of dancer and audience alike. The dancer of ancient South Asia studied the embodiment of *rasa,* that is, how to convey with her body the essence of the nine *rasa*s, not as she individually felt them but as transcendent themes of aesthetic expression. It is through the experience of the *rasa*s that the rasika, the enlightened observer, might approach the highest levels of understanding that Hindu tradition embraces.

Such a dancer was not simply studying footwork, mudras, music, rhythm, and the stories that form the language of her dance. She was studying the embodiment of a cultural tradition. She had learned, kinesthetically, the very essence of that ancient culture. She could feel and project, in a language that goes beyond mere words, its value and its strength.

The Nrithyanjali Dancers portray the eight *rasa*s in a Bharata Natyam form.

FIGURE 3.6A *Shringara,* love.

FIGURE 3.6B *Hasya*, humor, the comic.

FIGURE 3.6C *Karuna*, pathos.

FIGURE 3.6D *Raudra*, anger.

FIGURE 3.6E *Vira*, heroism.

FIGURE 3.6F *Bhayanaka*, fear/panic.

FIGURE 3.6G *Bibhatsa*, distaste, revulsion.

FIGURE 3.6H *Abdhuta*, wonder, surprise.

A classical temple dancer would have been steeped in her discipline over approximately a decade before performing her Arangetram, that first public appearance. It is important to note that the English word "discipline" is derived from the same root as the word "disciple." It translates quite nicely the essence of the student-guru relationship in a process designed to achieve a spiritual goal of understanding.

The traditional form of transmission, the gurukulam, was the setting for the guru-shishya relationship. A future dancer would move into the home of her guru, to serve her master and to absorb not only the technique but also the sensibility of the dance, its history, its aesthetics, and its purpose. She would learn a lifestyle and how to manage it. The relationship to the guru is frequently described as one of service; the purpose and design of this level of dedication also prepared the future performer for her relationship to the art form: "the respect, obedience and service rendered to a guru are meant to break down the ego until gradually the ego subsides and the true self emerges fully."[12] That "true self" in Indian philosophy is the divine self, that aspect synonymous with the divine essence. Ultimately, a dancer's goal was to be dedicated to a temple or to a royal court. Whether she were dedicated in this way to the deity presiding over a temple, to a ritual object, or to a raja presiding over a court, she would be considered to be in a relationship of consort or marriage, and unable to marry another. She was, however, able to bear children, who would then join the hereditary group of performers.

The dancers came from a particular and hereditary population, the *devadasis*, as is traditionally the case in most performing arts, most fine arts, and indeed most vocations in South Asia to this day. Not so much a caste or even a subcaste, strictly speaking, the devadasi community produced the dancers (mostly women) and their musical accompanists (mostly men) for centuries, preserving their unique style. The word "devadasi" itself is often translated "servant of god," since "deva" is always deity. But "dasi" may better be rendered as "consort" or even "spouse." A consort or spouse may, of course, serve, but not necessarily from a position of inferiority or weakness. She may be a partner. This relationship is not without sexual overtones, and that fact lies at the root of many of the difficulties associated with the devadasis. If the dancer were understood to have an intimate physical relationship with the divine, her body would be a living icon, a physical embodiment or container of the divine. If she were seducing the deity into her body, worshippers might consider contact with her to be very powerful. In the ancient world, temple prostitution arose from just these sorts of premises. If the dasi attam performers physically communicated this sensibility, we can easily imagine what Rukmini Devi feared, what the horrified British saw, and why the devadasis had such a bad reputation. But the relationship to the divine was actually symbolic in nature. T. Balasaraswati, the fierce defender of the traditional form of the dance, insisted that the shringara *rasa* (the *rasa* of love) was *never* intended to be perceived literally, and if the theory of *rasa* contained in the texts had been truly translated into the dance, it could not have been. Misapprehension occurred because the gestural language, the physical postures, and the facial expressions were misinterpreted by those who simply were not true rasikas. This, too, is easy enough to imagine.

An elaborate system of patronage existed to support this system. Devadasis were literate, educated, financially independent women, whose sexuality was a lively part of their identity. Under the best of circumstances, they may have been the most independent women in South Asia; under the worst, they were liable to be treated as property and were extremely vulnerable. This explains, in part, the legislation in 1947 outlawing the dedication of young women to temples. But other forces were in play as well.

Shringara Rasa: What Love Has to Do with It

If western religions continue to display a tortured ambivalence regarding their relationship to the performing arts, this reflects the underlying assumption that the performing arts, and particularly dance by females, have long been associated with eroticism. The association is not superfluous or gratuitous. In most traditional cultures, dance has its roots in rituals related to fertility, and those roots are deeply grounded. From maypole dances to swing, the sexual implications of the dancing body, male and female, are hard to ignore. For the West, this has proved problematic, and there are sects of western religions that prohibit dancing altogether. For the varied cultures of India, the issue apparently did not exist until influences and sensibilities from the West pervaded the subcontinent. The reasons are many and complex; for the purposes of this study, the focus is on this first and arguably most powerful *rasa.*

Shringara is usually translated as "love," and in the Indian context, this category of "flavor" includes passion, that is, the physical aspect of love. If one of the functions of performance is embodiment, that is, the joining of body and mind, then to acknowledge that physical passion is of paramount importance is natural and appropriate. There is no inherent judgment; it is simply a truism. Indian traditions have not only incorporated physical desire and experience in their aesthetic theory, they have embraced them. The reasoning is that if sexuality is responsible for life as we know it on the microcosmic plane, it must have its origins in the macrocosm, the divine realm, as well. And where the aesthetic goes, there also goes religion in India. There are many cosmologies in Hinduism, many accounts of the sources and origins of the world. These sometimes overlapping and often disparate myths are not understood as in conflict; rather, they complement one another. And since time is circular in Hindu thought, they are recurring as well. Creativity and fertility are understood as fundamentally sexual in nature. Creation is sustained by divine sexuality. It is not surprising in this context that the dancers associated with the temples of South Asia were understood to be participating in that sustenance sexually. We do not have extensive documentation of their role in the ancient world, but we certainly have texts and traditions rich in references to the centrality of erotic passion in the artistic and religious heritage. It is important to remember that sexual promiscuity has never been a major practice in traditional South Asian cultures; if anything, it is less prominent there than it has been in other cultures. The acknowledgment of the power of sexuality, then, has not resulted in behavioral responses among the general population. In part, this is a function of a strictly structured social context. But it is also a reflection of the ways in which India has understood the nature of physical, and therefore sexual, reality. All of these factors contribute to the nature and importance of shringara *rasa.*

South Asia is an inherently sensual milieu. The brilliant colors, the range of tactile and visual stimulants, the quality of movement, the sounds and smells and tastes that all combine to produce experience and response, and ultimately the arts, can lead to sensory overload for those unused to the intensity. The appreciation of those stimuli has led to an aesthetic that is well aware of the power that lies in sensuality and has sought the meanings and implications of that power. The same is true of sexuality. So it is that the walls of temples, the centuries of painting and sculpture, and the performers associated with those sacred spaces share some of the most erotic art that the world has seen. There is, inherent in Indian culture, a deep appreciation for these expressions of shringara *rasa*, as well as an enjoyment of their suggestive qualities and a wonderful sense of humor regarding the sexual exploits of both gods and humans. It has had to be masked often, and at times it has been driven completely underground by the attitudes of those who had no hope of understanding but had the power to suppress it.

There are many texts of poetry that explore the two types of shringara *rasa* elaborated by Bharata in the *Natyashastra*, "love in separation" and "love in union." One of the most famous examples in which these two aspects are explored is the *Gita Govinda*. In this remarkable work by Jayadeva, written in the twelfth century of the Common Era, the topic is the love affair between the divine Krishna and the mortal Radha, a theme celebrated throughout India for many centuries in ritual, festival, and all the arts. Their relationship forms the basis for bhakti devotionalism, the worship of Krishna as the immediate presence of God on earth. This is no "platonic" love affair, however: there is no doubt either in the text or in the many other traditions that celebrate their love that Radha and Krishna were physical lovers. As Lee Siegel has observed: "The religious experience of communion, of the 'supreme joy' and ineffable ecstasy of the two merging into one, 'without duality,' finds expression in terms of the sexual experience."[13] There is an entire genre of performance in India known as *raas lila* in which the love affair is played out in ritual, ceremonial, and playful ecstasy.[14] The elaborate celebration of the *Holi* festival in India and now in the diaspora communities emphasizes this merging of all dualities, male and female, human and divine, macrocosm and microcosm, with the use of dance, the use of colored water, the suspension of ordinary social inhibitions, and a healthy dose of sexuality as a running theme throughout.[15] This is a spring fertility festival, and the joining of Krishna with his human lover is a metaphor for the joining of heaven with earth, to produce life. In India, the physical act of love is part of that equation.

Frederique Apffel Marglin conducted research among Orissi dancers who were affiliated with the Lord Jagannatha (Lord of the World) Temple in Puri, Orissa, before the particular dance practices associated with that temple ceased. Her work produced fascinating results regarding the identity of the devadasis in the temple context and how their sexuality was transmuted. Based on information gleaned from this research, the role of temple dancers in a wider context may be better understood, although obviously not all conclusions may translate evenly, and it is always dangerous to generalize based on limited research, especially in a cultural climate as diverse as India's.

Marglin's approach to shringara *rasa* begins with an examination of the meaning of "emotion" in Indian experience. Whereas "erotic emotion" may appear to be a sensible translation of the Sanskrit, Marglin suggests that the western understanding of "emotion" is misleading in this context.[16] Rather, she offers the expression "embodied thought," coined by Michelle Rosaldo.[17] "When successfully carried out, the ritual enables the participants-devotees (the spectators as well as the performers) to experience the 'tasting of *shringara rasa*,' an experience at once physical, emotional, and cognitive."[18] Marglin also refers to Stanley Tambiah's theory and vocabulary regarding the transformation as the "performative outcome of ritual."[19] The index of the ritual's success is called its "transformative efficacy," and is "precisely the result of this integration of form and content."[20] The form, the gestural language, the structure of the dance, the physical edifice of the temple, and the physical form of the dancer herself become one with the content of the performance, the symbolic, transformative concepts that compose a unique relationship between deity and temple, temple and dancer, dancer and dance, dance and spectator. There is emotion, there is cognition, and both are "experienced and discussed as unified activity."[21]

Marglin's informants in Puri described the ceremony in which they were dedicated to temple service as a marriage to the deity Jagannatha, a local incarnation of Vishnu. Forbidden to marry any other, they nevertheless were able to have sexual relationships with mortal men, although bearing children was discouraged. They were often encouraged to have sexual relationships with the local raja or king, who, as a partial incarnation of Jagannatha, was understood to be strengthened by contact with the devadasis.[22] As consorts of the divine lord, they were understood as embodiments of his divine consort, Lakshmi, and as such, were associated with auspiciousness, fertility, wealth, and success: earthly feminine divinity. The marriage of Vishnu and Lakshmi is the marriage of heaven and earth. Contact with such a woman would have been considered a great benefit; there were precise rules regarding who was allowed access. Her very sexuality was considered fortunate, for it was associated with the fertility of the world. The success of the annual monsoon and the consequent success of the crops were believed to depend upon her benevolence and the power she inherently carried as a result of her identity and stature.

Marglin details many aspects of the temple dance rituals performed by the devadasis; it is clear that they were intended to bestow a multitude of blessings as a direct result of sexual identity and the eternal divine feminine power of *Shakti*. As for the women themselves, "the dancer's own transformation necessitates the muting or even erasing of her own subjective feelings." One of Marglin's informants stated, "A devadasi should have no attachment. A young woman will fulfill her desire for sex, but she should have no attachment." Marglin observes:

> This quite clearly shows that, even in their liaisons, the *devadasis* should not become attached. They always lived in their own houses and under normal conditions did not move to their lovers' houses: the *devadasi* is thus made into the effective vehicle of female divine sovereignty by her life-long unmarried status as well as by her training in the dance. (Frederique Apffel Marglin, "Refining the Body," 222)

> The *devadasi's* training and social position as a temple servant as well as the more immediate preparations she undertakes before dancing in the temple—purifying herself, dressing and decorating herself in a particular way—all amount to processes of refinement that transform her into "the mobile goddess." (Ibid., 223)

In other words, the temple dancer could form no attachments in an emotional sense, because to do so would compromise her ability to achieve and maintain the condition by which she could serve as a vehicle for the divine manifestation of *rasa*. As we have seen, *rasa* cannot be the projection of individual, personal emotion; similarly, shringara *rasa* cannot be the projection of individual, personal sexuality. If she was properly trained and processed, just as a savory dish is properly prepared, cooked, refined, her own personality was subsumed by the larger, macrocosmic reality. "The divinizing of the devadasi's body, her transformation, is the starting point for the transformations in the spectators."[23] Her dance is erotic, to be sure, because it is in its eroticism that the transformative, creative, generative power, its "tranformative efficacy," resides. But this is refined eroticism, on a level removed, processed, in fact, beyond the particular. "Should a spectator directly lust for the dancer, the performative efficacy of the ritual would have failed, and the erotic sensation would not be experienced as shringara *rasa* but as lust."[24] The process of refinement described above was not intended to disparage or discourage human sexuality or sensuality. Rather, it "implies that one starts with a concrete or physical or gross level and by successive processes of refinement extracts from these concrete emotions their essence."[25] That essence, in its ultimate state, is *rasa*.

Kathak

Like most classical forms of dance in South Asia, Kathak appears to have originated in temple-centered devotion. This dance form, however, has several unique characteristics, and its development has been dramatically influenced by the Muslim presence in the northern parts of the subcontinent. One distinction that seems to date back to its origins is the fact that the original *Kathakas*, like those described in the epic *Mahabharata*, were "story-telling Brahmins," who "belonged to that class of men whose work was associated with oral meditations in the sacred traditions."[26]

> Thus, it appears that Kathak, as the name suggests, originated in the Indus-Gangetic belt where the Brahmins (priests) while recounting stories based on Hindu mythology reached the point of ecstasy in their

devotion which manifested itself through the medium of dance. This dance form was called Kathak, derived from the word "Kathakar" (story teller) and "katha" (story). (Shovana Narayan, *Rhythmic Echoes and Reflections: Kathak*, 9)

Unlike other dance forms, therefore, Kathak has always been taught and studied by members of the highest caste. This trend continues today.

The arrival of Islam in northern India necessitated a metamorphosis, since the traditional Hindu stories highlighted not only a multitude of deities and the worship of icons but also the understanding of the dancer as a living icon. Sufism, the mystical dimension of Islam, was able to bridge some of the gap between the two religions by emphasizing ecstatic experience, and the role of dance and music in this aspect of religion is well documented. Together with bhakti forms of devotionalism that developed in India, the mystical strains of Islam and those of Hinduism found common ground. The result of this synthesis was a flowering of graphic, poetic, and performing arts characteristic of the Moghul period, particularly during the reign of Akbar in the sixteenth century.

> The themes of the dances were now no longer confined to the myths and legend of Hinduism. The wider repertoire included imperial, social and contemporary themes. In fact, under rulers less tolerant than Akbar, Kathak developed along purely secular lines. The dancers concentrated on brilliant variations of rhythm, the beauty of which was heightened by tantalizing pauses and lightning pirouettes. (Reginald Massey, *India's Kathak Dance, Past, Present and Future*, 18)

With the decline of the Moghuls, the dance fell into disrepute and became less connected to its mystical roots and more a form of courtly entertainment. Shringara *rasa* carries with it always the possibility of embodying the erotic at the personal level, certainly when its audience fails to comprehend its original sensibility. By the time Europeans arrived on the subcontinent, in the seventeenth century, and called the dancers they saw "nautch" girls,[27] it may well have been the case that the professional dancers had lost their way; but one must also attribute European attitudes to abundant ignorance. Despite all the negative perceptions, however, Kathak was so rooted in northern India that it survived. It is still the case that accomplishments in the arts are encouraged among high-caste Hindu women in Rajasthan and Bengal, for the appreciation of their families both before and after marriage.[28]

The *nritya* or interpretive/expressionistic aspect of Kathak has always been strong, as a result of the form's roots in storytelling. As is the case with Bharata Natyam and Kathakali, the dance usually proceeds from a sung story and rhythmic accompaniment. The dancer combines intricate footwork with facial expressions and the elaborate hand movements, called hastas and mudras, that characterize Indian dance generally.

> The words "hastas" and "mudras" are usually used as synonyms; however a "mudra" by itself conveys a meaning unlike the "hasta" which has to be seen in a context. But when able to communicate a meaning by itself, the "hasta" is usually referred to as a "hasta-mudra." (Narayan, *Rhythmic Echoes and Reflections: Kathak*, 70)

Kathak's characteristic pirouettes, as well as the compelling performative dialogue between the dancer and the musicians, especially the percussionist (called *sawal-jawab*, "question and answer")[29] distinguish it from many other Indian dances. There is even a form, called *thumri andaaz*, in which footwork is eliminated: the dancer performs sitting, using the hands, face, eyes, and upper body, with a shawl draped over the lower body.[30] Watching a performance by such an artist is an extraordinary experience. A single phrase of a song may be repeated, mesmerizingly, for hours, as the dancer plumbs the depths of its interpretation. This particular form has become rare for a variety of reasons, including the faster pace of life in India and the relatively small audiences for this highly expressive art form. Balancing this trend, Kathak has recently found a wider audience in the West as well as in India, and its dynamism is electrifying to audiences.

Because Kathak evolved bridging two very disparate religious traditions, Hinduism and Islam, and accommodating the sensibilities of both, it does not belong in the category of "secular" entertainment, despite

FIGURE 3.7 Parul Shah in a classic *Kathak* posture.
COURTESY OF PARUL SHAH

many attempts over time to classify it as such. It would be more appropriate to observe that while Kathak successfully transcended particular religious affiliations, it did so by reaching for and attaining *rasa* in its most elemental sense, as an experience of transformation of a spiritual nature, not confined by ideologies or theologies. Moreover, the songs that accompany a Kathak performance to this day are those that describe its mythological heritage, whether Hindu or Islamic in content or reference, and often refer to the legendary rajas who were patrons of the art form. Where kingship is understood as divinely inspired, the stories of kings partake of divine inspiration. Kathak also remains one of the best dance forms for the illustration of circularity in time in South Asian traditions, for those "lightning pirouettes" underscore the theme with undeniable effectiveness. As it increasingly finds an appreciative audience on the world stage, its traditional and classical nature becomes more explicit.

Kathakali

Far to the south and on the western coast of South Asia lies Kerala, an area dominated by its tropical climate and artistic spirit. As Tamil Nadu produced Bharata Natyam, Kerala produced Mohiniyattam and Kathakali, along with a variety of related dance forms. It also created a system of martial arts, Kalarippayattu, closely allied with these. While we cannot linger over this relationship, it is notable that the martial arts have flourished in India from ancient times, and that they share in large measure many of the forms and functions characteristic of dance, along with their spiritual implications. Many of the same skills are nourished in order to produce similar outcomes by concentrated effort, training of the body, and mental concentration. Phillip Zarrilli has characterized this form of practice as a mode of "embodied doing." He provides the following observation regarding training activities, using an ethnographic system of characterization developed by Mauss and de Certeau:

> Extra-daily practices are those practices such as rituals, dances, theatre performances, the recitation of oral narratives, meditation and/or religious practices, martial arts, etc., which require the practitioner to undergo spe-

cialized body training in order to become accomplished in attaining a certain specialized state of consciousness, body, agency, power, and so on. Extraordinary energy, time and resources are often invested by a society to create cultural specialists whose embodied practices are the means by which personal, social, ritual and/or cosmological realities are created and enacted. (Phillip B. Zarrilli, *When the Body Becomes All Eyes*, 5)

Kathakali, with its unique costumes and style, is a relatively recent development in classical Indian dance, probably dating "only" to the sixteenth or seventeenth century of the Common Era. Its predecessor, Krishnattam, was performed only for the gods, behind the walls of temples "as visual sacrifices/offerings," and for those of the highest castes.[31] Kathakali evolved to serve a wider audience. In its pure form, it was presented in marathon sessions that would last night after night for days on end. Like other forms of classical dance on the subcontinent, it was designed to tell the famous stories of the Puranas, the *Mahabharata*, and the *Ramayana* to audiences that already know them well. Watching these tales unfold in performance is not a matter of "finding out what happens"; rather, it allows the audience to explore in depth the multiple interpretations possible for every action and the subtleties within each character, and to reach, each in his or her own self, for the transcendent experience of *rasa*. Beyond its intrinsic aesthetic potential, the movements, props, and characterizations of this performance genre resonate with audiences because of explicit connections to ritual worship, for example of the goddess Bhadrakali.[32] Symbols and signifiers reinforce each other over a multitude of physical and imaginal locations, woven quite naturally into a tapestry of context. Everyday life—the rituals of personal, social, and economic behavior—is mirrored in formal and informal festival, ceremonial, and devotional settings. Religion does not exist apart from or alongside other categories of behavior; it is not separate but fundamentally interwoven.

Kathakali performers were traditionally all male; female impersonation was one of the challenges of the many years of training required to become a performer. As is true of Bharata Natyam, the preparation of the performer requires time and patience, but in this case the make-up alone may take many hours, and the costumes may weigh upward of fifty pounds.

FIGURE 3.8 Kathakali costume and make-up is detailed, extensive, and quite heavy. Above, an example of Katti ("knife") make-up used for Ravanna, the Demon King of Lanka in the *Ramayana*, worn by Padmanabhan Nayar.

The stamina necessary to sustain a full Kathakali offering is extraordinary, and the physical prowess required to move within the constraints of the costumes is considerable. The state of mind that makes this demanding art possible is attained through many years of training both the body and the mind; in fact, with Kathakali it is possible to wonder whether the separation implied by these distinguishing nouns even applies. If it is true that in Indian dance the body and the mind find not proximity, not resemblance, but identity, then it may be here, in this particular dance form, that identity is clearly manifested. This opens yet another window onto the mystery of *rasa*.

Not only are the body and the mind merged in the performer and performance; other perceived dualities are dissolved as well, as a result of the physical discipline of these art forms. "The goal of all such virtuosic systems is reaching a state of 'accomplishment' (*siddhi*) in which the doer and done are one. Through such actualized practice comes both control and transcendence of 'self.' " The practitioner "is absorbed in performing (doing) psychophysical acts which totally engage his body, mind, and spirit." Zarrilli describes this as an "encoding of body-consciousness." In fact, this process not only resembles a ritual process, "it is a ritual process. The result may be just as radical and effective a transformation of the individual as what occurs in healing or life-cycle rituals." For these disciplines assume that the training is "a psychophysical means to effecting a fundamental transformation in the individual."[33] The Kathakali actor learns the techniques of breath/energy control known to animate (enliven) life-force energies, similar to forms of yoga and meditation. In South Asia the source of these energies is Shakti, the archetypal feminine origin of all that lives and breathes.[34] There is an elaborate physiology of transformation involved in this process that is transmitted orally, kinesthetically, and with repeated practice and exposure. It requires, as do most of the spiritual and performing arts in traditional India, the suspension not of disbelief but of ego.

"The release of energy/life-force constituting the 'presence' of the performer is something objective and (ideally) separate from the ego-bound personality. . . . In such moments of release the performer is transparent, the medium for the other. His life-force is but one infinitesimal manifestation of the macrocosm."[35] The performer is the lens through which the larger, divine reality manifests itself. Far from being a step *away* from reality, as western performance is understood, this is a step into *ultimate reality*, more real than the smaller and considerably less significant microcosmic reality of human life and experience.

D. Appukuttan Nair and K. Ayappa Paniker, in their editorial introduction to *Kathakali: The Art of the Non-Worldly*, put it this way:

> Among the various performing arts in India, and perhaps, even the world, Kathakali is unique in so far as it is one of the farthest from earthly reality and humanism.
>
> That presentation, whether in form, colour, behavior, or sound, is deliberately made contra-human, to exist in another world: that of the imagination of the connoisseur. . . . *Kathakali* takes the connoisseur away from the transient worldly experience of pleasure to one of transcendental entrancement.

In the book's first chapter, "The Philosophy of Kathakali," Nair describes the

> ultimate goal of the rasika (here *sahridayan*), when he adds that only such a one may: experience bliss which is non-dual, at which level there is no difference between beauty and ugliness; it is the realm where art and anti-art co-exist. . . . This point of bliss is also the level of divine art—that is, art beyond art. . . . The dualistic realm of art is not pleasing to a philosopher appreciator. The supreme *sahrdayan* seeks the non-dualistic variety of art, where the artiste, the art-form, and the connoisseur become one.

Phillip Zarrilli's work explores the dynamic relationship Kathakali establishes between the performer and the performed through the psychophysical discipline attained over years of training, practice, and exposure to the form. It is well to remember in this context that "psyche," the root of "psychology," is the Greek word for soul. Psychophysicality, then, is the reunion of soul and body in a transcendent moment of experience. Kathakali offers a study not of religion *in* performance art but of

Expression of the *rasas* in a Kathakali form, with the addition of a ninth *rasa, shanta* or *santa,* and a tenth, *lajja,* shyness, one of three separate female expressions in the dance form. ALL PHOTOS COURTESY OF PHILLIP ZARRILLI

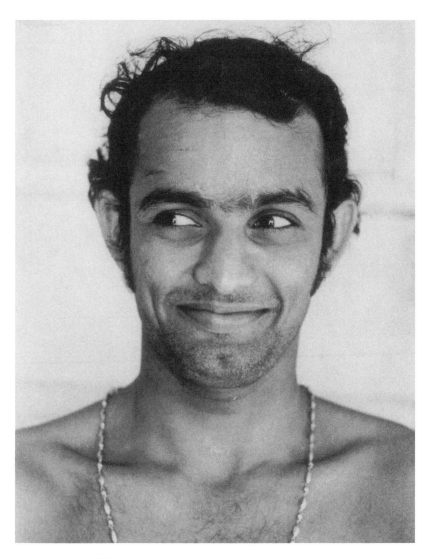

FIGURE 3.9A *Shringara,* love.

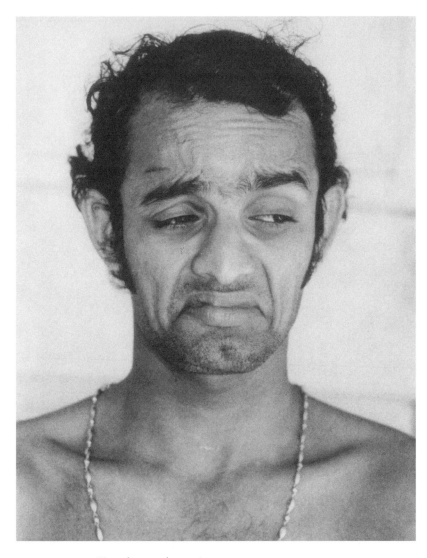

FIGURE 3.9B *Hasya*, humor, the comic.

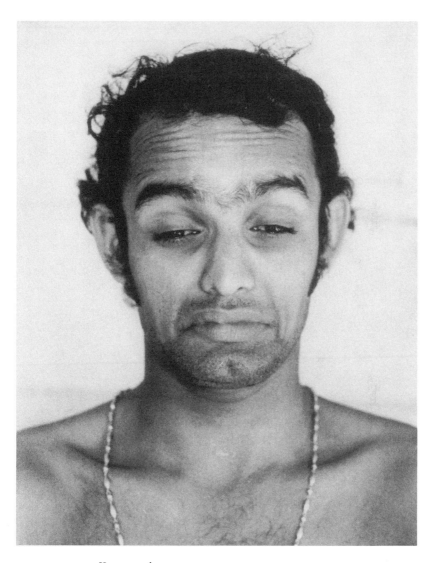

FIGURE 3.9C *Karuna,* pathos.

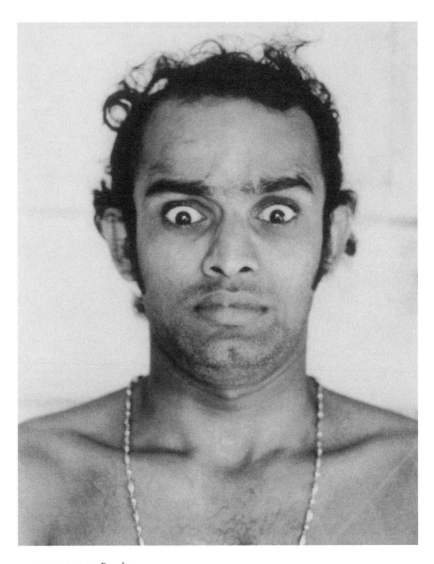

FIGURE 3.9D *Raudra*, anger.

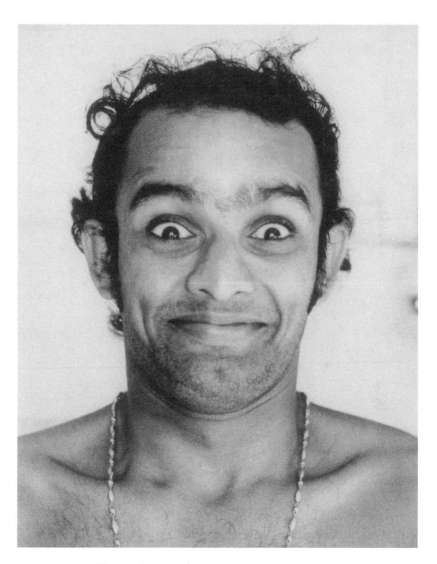

FIGURE 3.9E *Vira*, heroism.

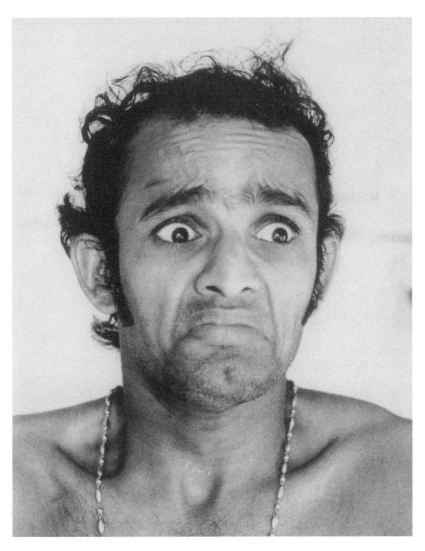

FIGURE 3.9F *Bhayanaka*, fear/panic.

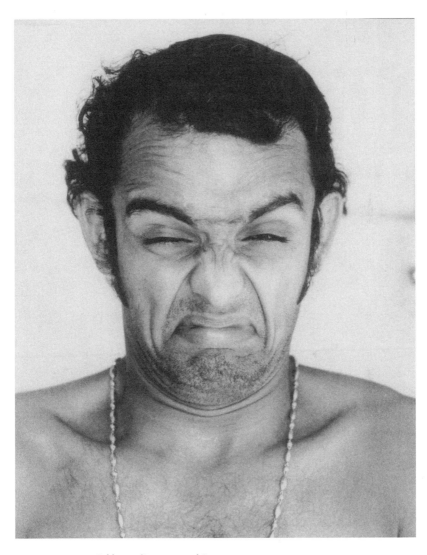

FIGURE 3.9G *Bibhatsa*, distaste, revulsion.

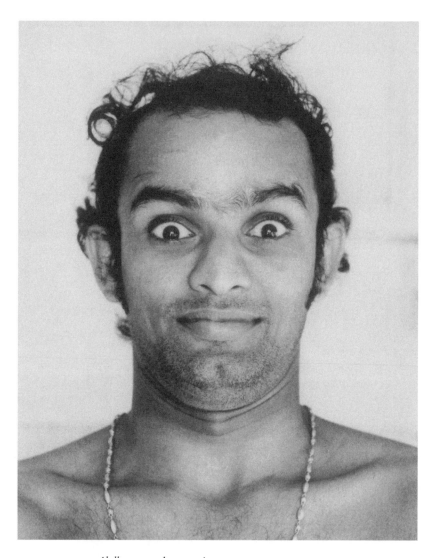

FIGURE 3.9H *Abdhuta*, wonder, surprise.

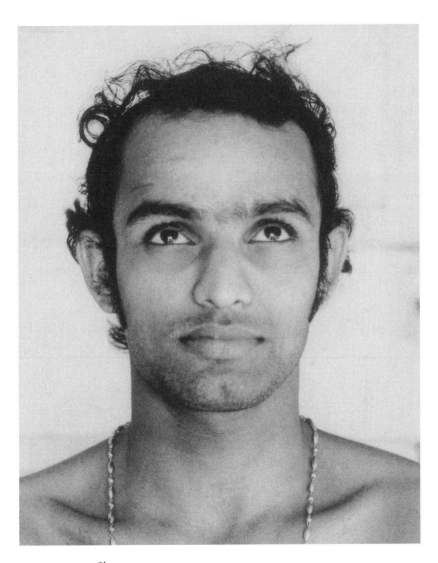

FIGURE 3.91 *Shanta*, peace.

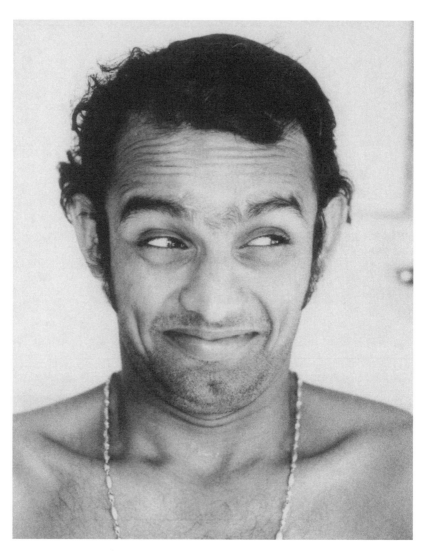

FIGURE 3.9J *Lajja,* shyness.

performance art *as* religion, philosophy, and psychology, all tangled up together. All comfortable western boundaries disappear and are replaced by an experience that defies categorization, and in so doing provides the living embodiment of *rasa*.

Arundhati Roy, in her exquisite novel of Kerala, *The God of Small Things*, gives a sensitive and heartbreaking description of Kathakali and its artists in contemporary India. The performers in this story offer a traditional nighttime ritual enactment to the gods as a way of attempting to atone for the necessarily superficial version of their art they must offer now, to audiences of tourists, nonrasikas all.

Kathakali discovered long ago that the secret of the Great Stories is that they *have* no secrets. The great Stories are the ones you have heard and want to hear again. The ones you can enter anywhere and inhabit comfortably. They don't deceive you with thrills and trick endings. They don't surprise you with the unforeseen. They are as familiar as the house you live in. Or the smell of your lover's skin. You know how they end, yet you listen as though you don't. In the way that although you know that one day you will die, you live as though you won't. In the Great Stories you know who lives, who dies, who finds love, who doesn't. And yet you want to know again.

That is their mystery and their magic.

To the Kathakali Man these stories are his children and his childhood. He has grown up within them. They are the house he was raised in, the meadows he played in. They are his windows and his way of seeing. So when he tells a story, he handles it as he would a child of his own. He teases it. He punishes it. He sends it up like a bubble. He wrestles it to the ground and lets it go again. He laughs at it because he loves it. He can fly you across whole worlds in minutes, he can stop for hours to examine a wilting leaf. Or play with a sleeping monkey's tail. He can turn effortlessly from the carnage of war into the felicity of a woman washing her hair in a mountain stream. From the crafty ebullience of a rakshasa with a new idea into a gossipy Malayali with a scandal to spread. From the sensuousness of a woman with a baby at her breast into the seductive mischief of Krishna's smile. He can reveal the nugget of sorrow that happiness contains. The hidden fish of shame in a sea of glory.

He tells stories of the gods, but his yarn is spun from the ungodly human heart.

The Kathakali Man is the most beautiful of men. Because his body *is* his soul. His only instrument. From the age of three it has been planed and polished, pared down, harnessed wholly to the task of storytelling. He has magic in him, this man within the painted mask and swirling skirts.

But these days he has become unviable. Unfeasible. Condemned goods. His children deride him. They long to be everything that he is not. He has watched them grow up to become clerks and bus conductors. Class IV nongazetted officers. With unions of their own.

But he himself, left dangling somewhere between heaven and earth, cannot do what they do. He cannot slide down the aisles of buses, counting change and selling tickets. He cannot answer bells that summon him. He cannot stoop behind trays of tea and Marie biscuits.

In despair, he turns to tourism. He enters the market. He hawks the only thing he owns. The stories that his body can tell.

He becomes a regional flavor. (*The God of Small Things*, 219)

GOOD TASTE IN MUSIC

Indian music boasts as long a history as dance and drama on the subcontinent, and its roots lie similarly in religious practice. While western forms of religion continue to experience the same tortured ambivalence about the use of music in sacred spaces as about dance, the cosmological power of sound acknowledged by Hindu tradition has ensured its high profile in all aspects of Indian life. Similar in many ways to dance, South Asian music appears to have begun in the temples and radiated outward to permeate every corner of Indian cultural expression. Any culture that acknowledges *mantra* (oral/aural sacred verse) as the "seed" of the world and acknowledges *Vac* as the divine feminine form of "voice," "word," "sound," and "being" is bound to place music at the center of its universe. Vac negotiates ambiguous territories among undifferentiated potentiality, formlessness empowered to become form, and manifestation or consciousness. Since Vedic times and likely before, the ritualist in India utilized sound to achieve identity with the divine, in a partnership to sustain creation.

As Andre Padoux has written, "we deal here with a set of facts and images where the mental, the phonic-phonetic, the physical, and the cosmic are thoroughly interwoven."[36] Sound not only affects life, it *effects* life, calls it into being. In describing South Indian danced texts, Saskia Kersenboom writes:

> Tamil verbal art is very much rooted in sound, and thus, in the skilful, imaginative rendering of that sound. Without that skill, which means a practice, and, implicitly, a way of life, no understanding, interpretation or appropriation is possible at all. (*Word, Sound, Image*, 88)

Music is part of a vast complex of factors that defines the South Asian "aesthetic universe." "Within a musical society that looks first to the past for guidance, making valid music is an affirmation of one's cultural identity."[37] Indian tradition has defined the style of its music with precision and typically exhaustive detail over many centuries, in texts and in oral transmission. It has used gendered language and gender-differentiated applications in that process.[38] The articulated function of the creator of music will by now sound familiar:

> The job of the composer is not to produce what brings particular delight to him; it is to produce what brings general delight to everyone. If he is able to surmount his personal desires and dislikes, the whole universe of art is open to him. (Lewis Rowell, *Music and Musical Thought in Early India*, 302)

Other criteria include level of refinement, as we would expect, in which the village performance is viewed as less worthy than one located in another venue. As we have seen, colors play an essential role in helping to define elusive qualities within Indian art forms; this is certainly true in music as well. Lewis Rowell offers the following schema:

FIGURE 3.10 The Goddess Saraswati holds her musical instrument, the *vina*. She is closely associated with music, voice, and poetry, and the knowledge and wisdom they contain. LIZABETH GOLDSWORTHY

FIGURE 3.11 Lord Ganesh is known as much for his music as for his dance.
LIZABETH GOLDSWORTHY

FIGURE 3.12 Krishna's flute accompanies the dances of the *gopis*, and is the call to those who worship him. LIZABETH GOLDSWORTHY

> *Rakta*: (red, impassioned), *surakta*: (well reddened, deeply colored), and
> *vicitra* (variegated, multi-colored) all suggest poetic enhancement
> through the use of color. This is easy enough to understand in a land with
> . . . a concept of decoration as an essential component of beauty, a sophis-
> ticated tradition of spices in cuisine, and sell-established preferences for
> bright, vivid colors. (*Music and Musical Thought in Early India,* 307)

It is clear that the voice was given primacy in musical tradition. Bharata
and his successors articulated a variety of criteria by which good voice
should be judged, including volume, sweetness, ability to shine in three
registers, ability to inspire pathos, rich coloring, and so forth. Similar criteria apply to instrumental performance.[39] All of these qualities are delin-
eated in the attempt to provide the musical path to *rasa*, which may be
defined in this context, in Rowell's words, as "a transcendent mode of
emotional awareness by which all aspects of a performance are integrated,
an awareness that rises above the circumstances which awakened it . . . and
generalizes the individual emotional states of the spectators into a single
emotional 'field.'"[40] As has been observed in the context of dance, this
field has the potential to provide in "the experience of art . . . a liberation
from constraints, moksha."[41] Just as the *rasas* are associated with particular postures and movements in dance, they correspond to the tonal notes
of emphasis in a musical composition along with other determining factors for tonal progression.[42] Rowell lists the following general criteria that
the tradition offers for the qualities of individual musical performance:

1. flawless
2. adorned rather than plain
3. refined, a category that includes both precision and delicacy, with negative
   value attached to the vulgar, harsh, rough or careless
4. continuous, in the form of a smooth, even, compact, connected, viscous
   stream of sound, with serene equilibrium as a goal and the process of
   creation as a model
5. appropriate (*aucitya*, an important category in Indian poetics) with reference to the relationship between sense, sight, and sound

6. intense, a category of value that includes the colorful, vivid, bright, radiant, illuminated, and impassioned, with negative value assigned to anything that is thin, bland, pallid, or dull

7. plastic, in the sense that it reveals the vital force that animates all life, as demonstrated in graceful, linear configurations, with negative value attached to the static, lifeless and awkward

8. evocative, in that it suggests more than the explicit content, flooding the senses with meaning

9. abundant and richly fertile, with negative value assigned to what is dry, parsimonious, fragile, strained or limited

10. clear in projection of the text, with crisply enunciated syllables

11. integrated and organically unified in an orderly manner, not disordered, broken, disjointed, or chaotic

12. comprehensive, in that the artistic contents are processed in a complete and systematic manner

—(*Music and Musical Thought in Early India*, 335)

Obviously, some of these refer to musically rendered texts, and it is important to remember that chanting the revered stories of India's rich heritage is common practice still. Pure musical performance has held its own as well, however. These criteria offer a rich area for consideration. Rowell emphasizes the value placed upon "the way in which nature works, pure, natural *process*: the demands for continuity (the way of creation), plasticity (the way of life), and abundance (the way of all nature, at least under ideal circumstances)." He also argues that beauty, that is, the achievement of *rasa*, is, according to these guidelines, an "*epiphany*, a manifestation of the light of creation to the senses, bringing the taste of delight and a glimpse of the ultimate in sensible, graspable form."[43]

Dissonance, Assonance, Variation, Transcendence

Most historians agree that in the middle of the second millennium before the Common Era (ca. 1500 B.C.E.) the indigenous Dravidian population of South Asia came under the influence of tribal Aryans. The nature and degree of Aryan influence has become part of a larger debate, but its effects in the arts were doubtless considerable. Aryan cultural influence resulted in the evolution of Sanskrit, the classical language of the major theological, philosophical, and poetic texts of northern Hinduism. The interaction between north and south within the larger Hindu population, as well as interaction with Buddhists and Jains, generated tremendous creativity and the continued development of aesthetic understanding.

> Both are credited with carrying sculpture to new heights in their cave shrines and stone temples. From then on, decorative friezes, sculptures and icons depict gods, saints and royal patrons who delight in music and dance. Religious activity was no longer reflected in the arts. The arts themselves became an integral part of religious activity. Participation in the arts, or at least artistic appreciation, began to define the individual's real identity on a metaphysical scale. (Ludwig Pesch, *The Illustrated Companion to South Indian Classical Music*, 37)

Later, the arrival of Islam beginning in the eighth century of the Common Era was to have strong impact as well. In the northern parts of the subcontinent where this influence was strongest, considerable change was wrought upon forms of artistic expression, especially music, which evolved toward "Hindustani" tradition, a blend of Hindu and Muslim influences, whereas southern or "Karnatic" traditions remained relatively distinct. These two major types of musical expression, however, did interact over time. And although the arts themselves may have been interpreted along different lines by Hindus and Muslims, patronage was a great sustaining force behind the continued existence and evolution of performing arts at the Moghul courts.

For the gurus and their shishyas, the process of studying classical music has long been understood as spiritual. Donna Wulff observes, "Especially in the South, but also among Hindu and Muslim musicians in the North, music, like all learning, has traditionally been regarded as a sacred endeavor."[44] "Indeed, the classical musician in India has traditionally been esteemed as a sort of 'priest' or conduit."[45] From the worship by teachers and students of the Goddess Saraswati, the divine essence of music and

FIGURE 3.13 The staccato rhythms of India's *tabla* music blur the hands of Shafaatullah Khan. JEDEDIAH BAKER

Opposite page:
FIGURE 3.14 A selected few of India's many musical instruments, left to right: tabla (*dayan*—treble drum—on top, and *bayan*—bass drum—on bottom); *dilruba* with bow; *tanpura*; *sitar*; *surbahar* (bass sitar, invented by Ustad Sahabdad Khan). JEDEDIAH BAKER

FIGURE 3.15 Some tools of the trade, clockwise from left: *powder-ki-dibya* (powder box for tabla); *hatodi* (hammer for tuning tabla); *mizrab* (plectrum for playing sitar); *tel-ki-dibya* (oil container for index and middle fingers of the fretting hand of the sitar). JEDEDIAH BAKER

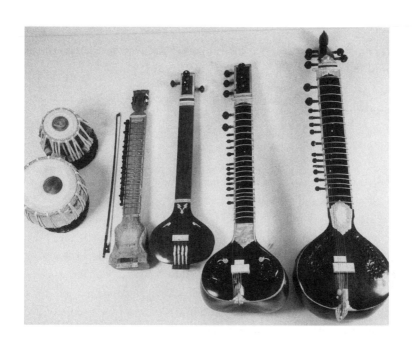

poetry who plays the stringed instrument called *vina*, to the special treatment of instruments or texts with regard to ritual purity, to the consecration of practice and performance spaces, the association of music and music making to divine action and manifestation is clear. Wulff quotes Ravi Shankar in his autobiography *My Music, My Life* as he verbalizes the special nature of this relationship:

> Our tradition teaches us that sound is God—Nada Brahma. That is, musical sound and the musical experience are steps to the realization of the self. We view music as a kind of spiritual discipline that raises one's inner being to divine peacefulness and bliss. We are taught that one of the fundamental goals a Hindu works toward in his lifetime is a knowledge of the true meaning of the universe—its unchanging, eternal essence— and this is realized first by a complete knowledge of one's self and one's own nature. The highest aim of our music is to reveal the essence of the universe it reflects, and the *ragas* are among the means by which this essence can be apprehended. Thus, through music, one can reach God. (*My Music, My Life*, 17)

It is notable that Shankar's primary guru (and future father-in-law), Allaudin Khan, was Muslim. It is through music that dialogue between Hindus and Muslims has often been possible. Muslim musicians will still say that this dialogue proceeds from Sufism, the same form of Islamic practice that in western Asia produced "whirling dervishes" and other examples of performed mystical engagement.

> That music is a means of devotion is perhaps the most common idea expressed by musicians. For Sufis and the Muslim musicians today, music as a form of devotion to and worship of God is the rationale given to explain the performance of music in the light of its discouragement or prohibition in Islam.
>
> Interestingly enough, although music and God are closely connected, music and religion are not. That is, all musicians, whatever their particular religious background, agree that one's personal religion has no effect on the performance of music. (Daniel M. Neuman, *The Life of Music in Northern India*, 60)

Daniel Neuman has even found that in the opinion of at least one of his informants, standard forms of religiosity might in fact impede "perception of Supreme Being through music," since "all musicians have one religion, music, and . . . a religious man cannot also be a musician."[46] The perception that institutionalized or organized religion is an impediment to the more generalized "spirituality" sought and experienced in the arts is increasingly an issue in South Asia, as we have seen is the case in the dance world.

Among gurus and shishyas, the devotion to music tends to overshadow other affiliations, sometimes to exclude them. Many stories about the traditional gurukulam system suggest that the intensity of the commitment and the methods of transmission parallel entrance into spiritual discipleship, and that the absorption of much more than structure and technique is involved. Ravi Shankar's own most famous western disciple is, of course, the late George Harrison. Harrison wrote in *Raga Mala,* Shankar's most recent autobiography:

> The guru-shishya relationship is an exceptionally powerful one, at the center of which is the one-to-one oral teaching method. In order to gain the benefits of the received wisdom of the ages, the student must yield completely to the demands of the guru in a submission of the ego, must accept without question what he is taught. Even more important than achieving technical proficiency (thought that is vital as well) is the process of imbibing direct from the guru the essence of each raga, and the essence of the music as a whole; without the feeling for these, his potential for authentic improvisation will always be limited. The relationship is as much spiritual as worldly, for the guru leads the pupil into the euphoria that results from true mastery of the music and appreciation of its transcendental potential. (*Raga Mala,* 85)

The "transcendental potential" of music is particularly powerful and suggestive in the Indian context. Indian musicians perform units of music known as *ragas,* predetermined melodic, tonal, and rhythmic themes associated with moods, times of the day, months, and years. Within the structures of those melodic units, the artist is given opportunity to explore, expand, improvise. It is by the ability to master the ragas and then

FIGURE 3.16 Shafaatullah Khan, center, in a typical sitar performance stage arrangement with his students, Sanjoy Biswas, tabla, left, and Nikita Pandya, tanpura, right.
JEDEDIAH BAKER

improvise upon them that the degree of proficiency is judged; that is, the musical form invites transcendence of its own structure. What is "in tune" is also, in the spiritual sense, "intoned." Ragas are believed to be organic, that is, living beings. Their perceptible form becomes manifest as a result of spiritual discipline. "A successful interpreter of a particular melody is complimented on having persuaded the deity of the raga to descend and reveal its sound-image, to live in his song or instrument."[47] Beryl De Zoete provides this wonderful story:

> It is told of Narada, who was a sort of Indian Orpheus, inventor of the vina and chief of heavenly musicians, that he caused a good deal of suffering to musical spirits, in the course of acquiring perfect mastery of his instrument. As we should put it, he "murdered" the music. Krishna, the divine flautist, a friend of Narada, devised a way of bringing this home to the sensitive musician. He took him to heaven in which many nymphs and angels sat weeping and in great pain. Narada was horrified at the sight and rushed forward to help them. But he was told that these were the very ragas and raginis whose limbs he had torn and mangled in his clumsy efforts to force their living forms to enter his melodies. Their spirits, he was taught by this sad demonstration, cannot safely descend from their celestial abode to live in their physical sound-forms unless the musical vehicles are perfectly shaped to receive them and delineated with the utmost perfection of technique as well as spiritual vision. (*Other Mind*, 31)

That music is capable of transcending boundaries both cultural and geographical is well known. Its ability to transcend the illusion of the world is what locates it center stage in Indian performing arts. That it can also transcend religious boundaries in the highly charged religio-political atmosphere of South Asia is particularly compelling. So many possibilities for transcendence reside in the cumulative traditions of India that music's exalted position in the culture is not surprising.

In traditional India, causal sound (*nada*) is closely related to the ultimate reality of Brahman. The term has been variously used to denote the primordial sound that animates the universe, as a general word meaning sound, as a descriptive term for the flow of vocal sound from within the body, and as a specific reference to the improvisation of a specific raga in performance.[48] It is clearly an active, generative force, hence its connection with Brahman. The thirteenth-century text of the *Sangitaratnakara* ("Ocean of Music") articulates this association by describing the major deities Shiva, Vishnu, and Brahma as essentially sound, and accessible through the worship of sound.[49]

Beyond providing devotional access to the divine realm, that is, the ability to invoke divine presence, music may provide the ultimate form of transcendence and transformation as defined by Indian thought. If the goal is to leave ego behind, negate the individual in favor of the universal, realize the final and complete unity of all of the manifestations that make up the world we recognize, music is a powerful means to that end. The musician who is completely at one with the music and the audience that is drawn into the "sound" of that unity transcend the boundaries of ego, and other boundaries as well. "Such a state of absorption is commonly experienced as a form of union, whether with the reality made manifest in the music . . . or with the One conceived . . . as its ultimate recipient. The musician . . . is therefore understood to exemplify and make available to an audience a profound spiritual experience."[50] The nature of that experience is beyond unity: it is identity. *Rasa* in music is the achievement of that transcendent goal. "Religion and art are thus names for one and the same experience—an intuition of reality and of identity."[51]

4

Transformations in Time and Space

A young woman stands before the audience on a proscenium stage in sub-urban Pennsylvania, highlighted by electric spotlights. The sound system is adjusted to maximum amplification. Live musicians, who often visit from India, sit in traditional posture with their instruments. Present as well on this auspicious occasion is her guru, who has helped her prepare for this moment over years of training in the sacred language, verbal and kines-thetic, of those ancient and evolving South Asian dance traditions. The words and the meaning of the lyrics sung by the accompanying musicians, the inflection and the posture of her presentation, and the long history of her people are all somehow contained in what she is about to perform. Far away in time and place from where it all began, the ancient and profound content of her action still carries importance. Before her are her extended family, parents, siblings, grandparents, uncles, aunts, and cousins, some of whom have traveled from India, waiting expectantly. Her friends are also present, and there may well be others: teachers, family friends, and experts in the area of expertise she has studied to prepare for this moment. Their expectation is flavored by ethnicity, tempered by geography, strengthened by the challenge of change and adaptation in a transplanted community. She stands and bears witness to both continuity and change. What are the parameters of her witness, how are they to be defined?

Arangetram, as discussed above in chapter 2, is the Sanskrit term that describes the moment when a young dancer, traditionally of Bharata Natyam, literally "takes the stage," or the performance space, for her first public presentation. A young woman goes up, stands before her community and her family, and participates in a religiously charged activity that requires intensive preparation and education in traditional forms and content. In the diaspora context, location is both geographical and imaginal. It is easy to pinpoint where one dwells on a political map; where one dwells emotionally is always under negotiation. Adaptation may require major alterations in the way a community understands itself, not to mention how it understands the "homeland." The implications for rituals such as these are profound. Analytical tools across disciplines prove helpful in the attempt to understand what these young women may achieve, and what they may not.

The radical changes that occurred within the traditional temple dance tradition in India during the twentieth century have been extended and amplified among the diaspora Indian communities. The traditional devadasis faded from view with the deterioration of their support system. Efforts were made to establish independent and self-supporting dance academies to educate a growing number of young women in a variety of Indian dance traditions, particularly Bharata Natyam. The last great dancer from the traditional devadasi community, Balasaraswati, has spoken publicly and at length about the sacrifice of tradition in the process of this transformation.

Over the course of the twentieth century, it became possible, even fashionable, for upper-caste families to consider sending their daughters to study at dance institutes. Graduates were believed to have achieved both religious and artistic training, and to have become respectable embodiments of ancient tradition, albeit "ancient tradition" in a very altered sense of the expression. Performances outside of the temple context, on proscenium stages, became the norm. Young women with advanced training sought a different kind of economic sustenance in keeping with their own middle-class expectations and the expanding dance community both in and outside India: they discovered that by opening dance institutes they could sustain themselves and, in turn, their students could fan out and do the same. A quick tour of the World Wide Web will reveal that such institutions have multiplied exponentially, both virtually and actually, in the diaspora as they have in India, and that the Arangetram has become the showcase for the dance institute, its founding director, and Indian culture in its latest heterodox form. Training of young girls may begin with weekly lessons at age seven or eight, which increase in frequency as the debut performance approaches. The young woman's age at that time still varies, but the occasion's primary function remains: it is a measure of her expertise. While in the past this event would have been but a preliminary indicator of her prospects for a future vocation, now it is commonly viewed as a graduation ceremony, often featuring long and complex set pieces, diplomas, and gifts.

A controversial element of the modern Arangetram is that it is increasingly a showcase for affluence, and the spiraling cost of staging these performances has provoked considerable alarm both in India and in the diaspora. Invitations are becoming increasingly elaborate. Programs are typically printed, and may include graphics and photographs. These events may be held in school auditoriums, a development that raises the issue of holding a ceremony of a distinctly religious nature in a public space. But they may also be held in high-profile performance spaces, and costs easily escalate dramatically. It is common practice to include a dinner for guests after the performance. There is also the inevitable professional photographer and videographer, and elaborate jewelry and costumes (perhaps three changes during the performance), often brought from India. Notable differences in the tradition include: 1) the training and the ritual are now most likely to occur among middle-class and upper-caste Hindus; 2) the young woman and her family achieve status and visibility within the community as a result of engaging in this ritual; her marriagability may increase as well; 3) the dancer no longer trains exclusively for a vocation in dance; 4) a synthesized version of generic Hindu religious tradition is renewed and perpetuated for both participants and audience, a crucial function in the diaspora context. In many ways, the Arangetram provides both the proof and the support of what classical Indian dance has become. But what *has* it become? And what exactly has the young dancer become, having given her performance in this entirely new context?

How much religion is there in an Arangetram? The answer to this question in many ways encapsulates the problems of transition, both in the dance form itself and in the process of accommodating the diaspora. As Balasaraswati observed, for example, a dancer of Bharata Natyam in its earlier incarnations would rarely engage in a devotional display as part of her performance.[1] Her identity was enough to invoke the presence of the divine. An Arangetram in the "traditional" sense was a small occasion, attended by dance professionals who were well aware of the function of the dance's sacred nature. Acknowledgment of the guru was common, for the guru-shishya relationship has always been at the core of both the dance tradition in general and this ceremonial presentation in particular. This is still the case, to be sure: the young dancer will touch the feet of her guru at specified times during the program, the traditional form of acknowledgment, and offer gifts on stage. Currently, however, an Arangetram is also likely to feature not only icons on stage but also devotional worship at the beginning and the end of the performance. Add to this the fact that the actual content of the program incorporates the choreographed enactment of devotional songs and mythological texts, and the religious content cannot be missed. For young women of Indian but non-Hindu background, it is now possible to have an Arangetram performance dedicated to and enacting the narratives of Jaina *tirthankaras* (the twenty-four enlightened beings) and gospel accounts of Jesus. It appears that there is plenty of religion involved in this occasion. But what religion it is is less clear.

The Indian communities in the United States and elsewhere vary enormously, but in the current generation their visibility has increased with the construction of more traditional temples and community functions that attract interested participants from a variety of constituencies. Intermarriage has also had an impact, with the result that there are degrees of involvement across the spectrum. First- and second-generation U.S.-born Hindus, as well as Jains, Parsis, and Sikhs, often choose to send their daughters for classical dance instruction, should the community make it available by hiring a teacher or assisting in the opening of a dance institute. The expectation is that these young women will learn to perform at least to the level of an Arangetram, although few expect to become professional dancers or dance instructors. Far from the devadasi paradigm, these young women have the usual high professional aspirations in a variety of fields associated with their social and economic status in the diaspora; their "devotion to dance" is not primarily occupational. Rather, they and their parents see this endeavor as a "return to roots" and an education in "the traditions" of India.

Assimilation and secularization are a serious issue for the diaspora population, and the Bharata Natyam training and Arangetram performance are perceived as ammunition against those influences. The proliferation of symbols and ceremonial detail often proceeds with more fidelity to generic and popular perceptions of "Indian traditions" than to actual ancient and/or textually based practices of Hinduism. The increased visibility of icons on stage and devotional action directed toward them is designed to reinforce an idea of what Hindu practice might have required in some idealized past. The actual facts of devadasi traditions are usually not discussed, although most are aware that there was some sort of scandal associated with the dance form, in the days when girls were "given to dance."

As to whether the dance itself has been "sanitized" for presentation in this new venue, there is no doubt that much has changed. For while the dancer may portray the love of Krishna and Radha in her Arangetram, those trained abroad (and even some trained in India) rarely capture the sensuality that is arguably the most compelling characteristic of the story. It is precisely this quality that many argue has been edited out to grant respectability to Bharata Natyam in the postdevadasi scenario, so that it may survive and be perpetuated by the new breed of dancers with the support of their families. What is gained and what is lost in such a process?

Magdelene Gorringe, involved in research on Bharata Natyam and the Arangetram in Great Britain, has observed that the change of audience from trained specialists to the extended family and friends who attend a modern debut of this kind in the diaspora has altered the very nature of the performance. Aesthetic excellence may take an inferior position under these circumstances, where confirmation of the dancer's effort, the teacher's dedication, and the family's support are primary concerns. She argues that "art should not only represent but should also transcend and challenge a culture. When it does not do this it can slip into propaganda. This is a still more urgent danger when the culture represented is no longer the living, day to day practice, but, as with Arangetrams . . . an idealized vision of a culture now left behind, which in fact no longer exists in India, if it ever did."[2] Moreover, Gorringe fears, with the tendency to fix both the program and the attendant ceremony more rigidly, there is a real danger that the affluent minority in the diaspora are determining that which the world will see and define as "Hindu tradition," a misrepresentation of remarkable proportions. These are controversial statements regarding volatile issues; their veracity and implications require further study.

The debate regarding Indian classical dance, the evolving identity of Bharata Natyam and the Arangetram, is properly located in postcolonial and orientalist discourse as well as in the history of religion, religion and performing arts, and ritual and women's studies. Anthropologist Kalpana Ram, who has studied the Indian communities in Australia, observes that "cultural transmission as a conscious project already bespeaks a break-down";[3] that is, when an immigrant community sets out to represent its heritage it has already registered a sense of loss. Definitions of Indian womanhood are constructed in the diaspora around images and behaviors that create for the young female a perilous course; families make the choice to educate their daughters (and not their sons) in so-called "classical dance" under a number of influences from within as well as from without. These constructions of identity, like others in the immigrant community, are more often challenged during trips "home" to India than they are in the new environment: "both immigrant parents and their (exasperated!) children find that their peers have a far more open attitude towards responding to new contexts, which may allow for a far greater degree of 'Westernization' than is permissible among those actually living in the West."[4] Because classical dance is understood "by a particular class of Indians—as a transmitter of what is most representative and prestigious about Indian civilization,"[5] particular notions of nationalism as well as notions of gender are at play in the decision to support the training of daughters.

This thorny complex of attitudes and associations, however, does not do justice to the power of the performance itself. Ram successfully demonstrates that more is carried by the dance performance than ideology. As a performative act that "*consumes* the spectator," classical Indian dance forms explore the experience of *rasa* through what Ram calls the "transformative powers of artifice." Quoting Bachelard, she explores the ability of dance to elicit "a synthesis of memory and imagination. To dance, but also to sing or recite poetry . . . is to possess the capacity to give presence to an entire set of emotions that are somehow inherent in the patterns of performance." The immigrant audience is transported beyond the visual image "in a heightened awareness of embodied apperception."[6] As a result, "the listening, the keeping of time with hands with the variable rhythms of the *tala* (beat, tempo), the appreciative shaking of the head and verbal noises of encouragement with which audiences of Indian concerts engage with the performance" all evoke a physical engagement with memory and imagination that are transformative.

Because *rasa* has as its goal not simply the representation or evocation of emotion but its genesis, its creation on stage, it summons a physical memory of how the body moves in India. In what Ram calls "the nritta and raga of immigrant pasts,"[7] body attitudes and styles are called forth and geography and location are transmuted by emotional texture and color, resulting in a "synaesthesia of the senses."[8] Like the sympathetic strings of the *sarod* or the sitar, which far outnumber the primary plucked strings, the body is stimulated in a profusion of places other than the eyes that see and the ears that hear. The body responds in patterns that are located in South Asia, whether that body be there or in Great Britain, Australia, North America. Internal or imaginal geography triumphs over the external. According to Ram, the proscenium setting, quite a contrast to the former temple or court location, actually intensifies the experience. Herein lies the "magic of the performance": it is an act of conjuring, and it is both fundamentally sensual and inherently religious, with or without the stage icon, with or without the devotional lyric, with or without the invocation of a religious heritage whose diffuse nature is impossible to confine.

How are we to understand an Arangetram that is performed in the diaspora? It occurs for a variety of sociological and economic reasons, it is part of an adaptive strategy, it proceeds from a tradition simultaneously ancient in some respects and very recent in others. The young woman has not simply been studying footwork, mudras, the music and rhythm so essential to this art, and the stories that form the language of her dance. She has also been studying the embodiment of a cultural vocabulary. That vocabulary includes *rasa*, from its specific and technical facets to its more philosophical and essential "flavor." These are transmitted to the student in established ways. Although it could be argued that a conflation of *rasa* with bhava may occur under the influence of bhakti, or that personal emotion may be emphasized more than may have been the case historically, such judgments are quite difficult to make in a radically different context. These are issues of transcultural and transhistorical significance whose resolution is elusive. Ideally, the dancer has learned, kinesthetically, both to embody and to project that which defies time and location to the same extent that it transcends the personal: *rasa*. She can feel, in a language that goes beyond mere words, its value and its strength, and if she is proficient, she may convey that to her audience. Her western middle school principal, who may well have been invited, or her non-Indian girlfriends may catch a sympathetic vibration. The very sound and inflection of the words, the rhythm, and the melodic line, together with the subtleness of gesture, transport the gathering to another place, out of time and out of mind. It may not mean anything one would like it to mean, or anything it has ever meant before. That it is meaningful, however, is unquestionable. That it is a creative act, on many levels, is beyond argument. She stands before the audience to bear witness to all of this, and more: to transcend boundaries geographical, imaginal, ideological, gendered, and of course, religious.

In India, as elsewhere in the twenty-first century of the Common Era, one of the most problematic areas for discussion is religion. South Asia takes its religions very seriously indeed, and they are often associated with political issues and desperate problems that have become magnified in the past century. For many, it seems that a more secularized culture might function more smoothly; for others, it seems that one religious tradition ought to have predominance. This conflict is not exclusive to India, of course. Issues of modernization and its apparently inevitable by-product, secularization, have provided plenty of fuel for anxiety worldwide.[9] Indian genres of performance art, as they struggle for audiences, for financial health, for a vision of their future at home and abroad, have undergone many transformations. Questions regarding authenticity and agency are closely related and particularly urgent in this context.

While there have always been issues of authenticity among the many different gurus and schools of interpretation in South Asia, after independence in 1947 the sheer scope of differing approaches has increased to a remarkable extent. This proliferation of artistic interest and practice has resulted in an explosion of creativity; it has also raised the subject of authenticity to the level of national (and international) debate. What, in the context of world culture, is "Indian dance," or "Indian music"? When Indians at home and abroad participate in the many new forms of "fusion" music as well as dance, to increasing critical acclaim and audience approval, what sorts of compromises do they make, and to what ultimate effect? Indian artists and critics have become particularly sensitive to western aesthetics' influence on South Asian art forms from architecture to dance and beyond. The heavy hand of colonialism caused untold damage to the arts in South Asia. It is arguably true that renewed western interest in Indian performing arts in the twentieth and twenty-first centuries continues to influence artists and their work. Added to this is the influence of NRIs (nonresident Indians) exploring these art forms abroad, then returning to the subcontinent to display the fruits of their creative work, causing a sort of feedback loop. Who are the agents of change, by what authority do they practice, how do the lines of power and influence flow?

Within India, many artists have questioned and challenged the various performing traditions. One outstanding example is the dancer/choreographer Chandralekha. "*Rasa* . . . becomes . . . in her down-to-earth language the 'capacity of an individual to be integrated with herself, with society and nature.'"[10] Chandralekha's concern with the empowerment of Indian women through her art has led this Bharata Natyam artist to explore dimensions of *rasa* at a remove from traditional interpretations, with dramatic and radical results. She has come to take "a stand against the divine origins and manifestations of dance."[11] Rejecting the specific association with Hindu tradition that has been definitive of Indian dance forms since antiquity, however, is not necessarily a rejection of the essence of *rasa*. For as we have seen, the term transcends specific religiosity, even religious categories of thought that may confine and limit its possibilities. Chandralekha's interpretation of *rasa* may make more sense in contemporary India than the narrow use of religious imagery and ritual used simply to preserve form or to make a political statement. These issues will no doubt continue to be of pressing importance for performers, critics, and other participants in the culture wars internationally for the foreseeable future.

The primacy of performance in India is certainly not exclusive to Hindu tradition; indeed, it permeates many dimensions of life across the perceived and actual divisions of religion, language, sociology, economics, and politics. In "a society as prodigiously diverse as the Indian Subcontinent,"[12] the perils and possibilities of this cultural sensitivity to performance are impressive. Analysis of the ways in which both classical and contemporary movements in the performing arts may influence as well as reflect what Rustom Bharucha has called the "imaginary" of South Asian identity is compelling and fruitful. An understanding of the sources and influence of these traditions, therefore, has applications that extend well beyond the purview of theater.

The particularly Indian aspects of the power of performance are derived from both the power of active seeing (darshan) and the transformative aspects of live sound (mantra and vac).

> Drama, among all the arts that use language, is notable for the totality and immediacy of its effect on a real audience, an effect conveyed through language but derived from more fundamental kinesthetic and empathetic modes of response to events witnessed. (Edwin Gerow in Miller, *The Plays of Kalidasa, Theater of Memory*, 57)

Most powerful and significant is the spiritual dimension of *rasa* in its internal and external manifestations and the experience of divine identity that becomes possible when these elements are harmoniously integrated. Richard Schechner's recent essay, "Rasaesthetics,"[13] is concerned with the significance of *rasa* in its Indian setting and its implications for theater in the West. As a long-time student of the *Ram Lila* of Ramnagar, Schechner has witnessed the sensibility and the embodied reality of *rasa* and has formulated an intriguing analysis. To summarize very briefly, he is concerned primarily with bodily geography, that is, the location of the *rasa* experience in the body. Because of its very tangible essence as a digestive process, Schechner wants to emphasize its movement in the digestive tract, "the belly," as opposed to more western theatrical settings in the eyes and ears. "What is outside is transformed into what is inside."[14] The experience is a "blending of theater, dance, music, food and religious devotion,"[15] and characterizes festivals throughout South Asia. The rasic goal of Indian performance, he maintains, is the genesis of a third entity between the performer and the audience: the experience of the transcendent, archetypal emotion.[16]

As we have seen, *rasa* is *never* individual or personal sentiment, although these bhavas may be used to achieve it. A Kathakali dancer may or may not experience the *rasa* that he portrays. If he has trained properly, he is capable of projecting it completely so that it stands outside of himself, much as the gods in Hindu mythology create the world, and the simile is not accidental. Once it is "out there," the performer may, indeed, perceive it. More important, the rasikas (those educated in the "refined" tradition) or *bhaktas* (those whose preparation is more "devotional" than "classical"), the educated and prepared recipients of the performance, may have a moment of enlightenment and transcendence, and that is the ultimate purpose of the enterprise; the performance is a means to that end. The goal is to transcend the individual self altogether, not in favor of a character, which is merely another mask, but in favor of that third entity, that "other" projected by the artist's skill and inspired creativity. The ego is shed to spotlight that mysterious presence whose nature is divine. In this respect, religion *is* the performance, and the performance *is* religion, not in its characters or setting, its plot or content, but in its *essence*.

This is not "religion" in its institutional, denominational, political, or textual sense. In fact, it is not "religion" in accordance with any western theological model. Rather, it is an experiential phenomenon that may defy those normative constructs. In the West, this form of experience is now most often defined as "spiritual" in a very broad sense of that term. Its legitimacy and acceptability are very much a matter of debate. In India, however, its history is quite ancient, not as a term but as a sensibility, and it forms the basis of *rasa* in its most profound sense. As the principle underlying the form, content, and purpose of performance, it remains a compelling arbiter of artistic creativity. To what extent this aesthetic can survive the varied challenges of the present and future in the performing arts will be of compelling interest in India and in the world at large.

The very nature of live performance, its immediacy and its physicality, resists efforts to categorize or concretize its essence. Raising challenges and defying limitations, it offers a consistently radical mentality. *Rasa* may provide a uniquely Indian perspective on the nature of performance that resounds beyond geographical as well as religious boundaries. From Bharata's *Natyashastra* onward, the Indian approach to this inherently radical form of practice has been to identify and locate its power in the realm of religiosity. India's diffuse and diverse religiosity makes this approach to performing arts viable and unique. To the extent that music, dance, and drama retain that divine association, their rasic character continues to resonate and compel. Rather than being confined, limited, or narrowly defined by that sensibility, performance may be liberated. As much of India's philosophy insists, the ultimate goal of the transformative experience is the realization that the narrow confines of all systems are but maya, merely perception, illusion. To be sure, performance is a tenuous path to follow toward that goal, fraught with peril from within and without, from the considerable challenges of long and intense training to chronological, political, economic, sociological, geographical, and psychological pressures. But as the classical pose of Shiva Nataraja perfectly displays, between the creative and destructive forces stands the dancer, in perfect balance.

Glossary

ananda liberation from the self, realization of ultimate truth; the bliss and joy that result from such realization

Arangetram the debut performance of a dancer to demonstrate her ability

bhakta devotee of a deity; connoisseur of a performance whose purpose is to experience a divine spark

bhakti active devotion/service to a deity, usually involving ritual engagement

Bharata, Bharatamuni legendary author of the *Natyashastra*

bhava personal emotion that may be used to access transcendent *rasa*

bindu point or drop; a manifestation of creative energy and a source of creativity, structure, and dimension

Brahman the ultimate, supreme essence, formless and eternal

darshan the act of seeing and being seen by a deity

dasi attam dance form traditional in Tamil Nadu in the south of India that formed the basis of modern Bharata Natyam

devadasi a dancer dedicated or given to dance in association with a temple or court setting, and understood to enter into a special relationship with the divine source(s) of dance

dharma proper order, structure, behavior in and of the universe; the responsibility to uphold that sacred order and behave responsibly in accordance with its guidelines

diaspora a dispersion or "going out," usually from one's homeland

guru a master teacher of a spiritual discipline, including the fine arts

gurukula, gurukulam the home and family of the guru; setting in which a student became a member of the teacher's household in order to learn both the performance traditions and the way of life associated with them

hasta a hand gesture that, in a particular context of dance or other artistic representation, conveys a meaning

Holi annual spring festival celebrating the love between Krishna and Radha

lila play, in both the enacted dramatic and the ludic (playful, enjoyable) sense

mahagurus great and holy spiritual teachers

mandala a symbolic representation of the universe that may be two- or three-dimensional and is a focus of power

mantra a sacred formula, verse, or phrase intoned audibly or within oneself

maya the illusion that constructs and defines temporal experience and reality

moksha release from the cycles of rebirth, the ultimate spiritual goal

mudra a hand gesture that conveys a specific meaning

natya mimetic dance with a strong narrative line

nritta abstract, non-narrative dance

nritya mimetic (narrative) dance with an emphasis on rhythm

parampara traditions of dance and music taught to students

raga (m), **ragini** (f) the basic units of Indian music, a melodic framework, understood as masculine or feminine; comprised of set melodic phrases that are then interpreted and explored in performance; each is understood as eternal and divine

rajarasam quicksilver or mercury; highly valued substance used in alchemy

rasam Tamil equivalent of the Sanskrit *rasa*

rasika one who is educated and prepared to appreciate *rasa*

sahridayan one who is educated and learned

sanatana dharma the eternal and divine order of the universe

sawal-jawab the "question and answer," or performed interaction, between the drummer and the dancer in Kathak dance; for example, the drummer might perform a rapid and nuanced sequence of beats, and the dancer then duplicates them using her feet, hands, and postures

shakti ultimate energy and creative power associated with the divine feminine

shishya music or dance student under the guidance and tutelage of a guru

siddhi one possessing supernatural powers as a result of engaging in specialized spiritual and physical techniques

sitar a plucked string instrument similar to a lute, with movable frets and sympathetic strings

tabla a pair of drums prominent in Indian music; tabla or dayan actually refers to the right-hand drum, which is tuned; Baya is the left-hand drum, which is not tuned

tala tempo, beat, rhythm

Tirthankaras the twenty-four "enlightened beings" or Jinas who were the founders of Jainism and established the Jaina community

yugas the four major ages of creation, stretching over eons of time, that begin with a perfect world (*krita*) and decline through the *treta, dvapara,* and *kali.*

vac, Vac divine speech; the Goddess of divine speech

vina, veena long-necked string instrument, similar to a lute

Notes

1. A Taste of Things to Come

1. See for example Matthew Harp Allen, "Tales Tunes Tell: Deepening the Dialogue Between Classical and Non-Classical in the Music of India," *Yearbook for Traditional Music* 30 (1998): 22–52.

2. Rosemary Jeanes Antze, in Eugenio Barba and Nicola Savarese, *A Dictionary of Theatre Anthropology*, (New York: Routledge, 1991), 31–33.

2. *RASA* IN THEORY: TEXT AND CONTEXT

1. R. S. Khare, *The Eternal Food: Gastronomic Ideas and Experiences of Hindus and Buddhists* (Albany: State University of New York Press, 1992), 168.

2. Ibid., 169.

3. Saskia C. Kersenboom, *Word, Sound, Image, The Life of a Tamil Text* (Washington, DC: Berg Publishers, 1995), 227.

4. For example, see Michael W. Meister, *Cooking for the Gods* (Philadelphia: University of Pennsylvania Press, 1995).

5. Khare, 180.

6. Khare, 180–181.

7. F. Max Müller, the famous nineteenth-century German scholar, used the term "kathenotheism" to describe this form of belief.

8. See William S. Sax, ed., *The Gods at Play: Lila in South Asia* (New York: Oxford University Press, 1995).

9. Lewis Rowell, *Music and Musical Thought in Early India* (Chicago: University of Chicago Press, 1992), 180–181.

10. Kapila Vatsyayan, *Bharata: The Natyashastra* (New Delhi: Sahitya Akademi, 1996), 106.

11. Ibid., 58.

12. Ibid., 59.

13. Ibid., 62.

14. Ibid., 103.

15. Ibid., 112.

16. Ibid., 146.

17. Balwant Gargi, *Theatre in India* (New York: Theatre Arts Books, 1962), 12.

18. Bharata-Muni, *Natyashastra*, Vol. I and II, trans. Manomohan Ghosh (Calcutta: Granthalaya Private, Ltd., 1967), 6, 34–38.

19. Vatsyayan, 151.

20. Vatsyayan, 153.

21. Vatsyayan, 155.

22. Vatsyayan, 160.

23. Donna Wulff, "Religion in a New Mode: The Convergence of the Aesthetic and the Religious in Medieval India," *JAAR* LIV (4): 674.

24. Ibid., 677.

25. See for example Donald S. Lopez Jr., *Religions of India in Practice* (Princeton: Princeton University Press, 1995), 29–30.

26. David Kinsley, *The Divine Player: A Study of Krsna Lila* (Delhi: Motilal Banarsidass, 1979), 154–155.

3. *RASA* IN PRACTICE: DRAMA, DANCE, MUSIC

1. Farley P. Richman, Darius L. Swann, and Phillip B. Zarrilli, *Indian Theatre, Traditions of Performance* (Honolulu: University of Hawaii Press, 1990), 47.

2. Ibid.

3. Balwant Gargi, *Theatre in India* (New York: Theatre Arts Books, 1962), 6.

4. Barbara Stoler Miller, ed., *The Plays of Kalidasa, Theater of Memory* (New York: Columbia University Press, 1984), 19.

5. Edwin Gerow in ibid., 43.

6. See Gargi, chapter 1.

7. Miller, 30.

8. Miller, 14.

9. Shanta Serbjeet Singh, ed., *Indian Dance: The Ultimate Metaphor* (Chicago: Art Media Ltd., 2000), introduction.

10. Stella Kramrisch, *The Presence of Siva* (Princeton: Princeton University Press, 1981), 440. See also Paul Younger, *The Home of the Dancing Sivan* (New York: Oxford University Press, 1995).

11. Shovana Narayan, *Rhythmic Echoes and Reflections: Kathak* (New Delhi: Roli Books Pvt. Ltd., 1998), 54–55.

12. As related to Rosemary Jeanes Antze in Eugenio Barba and Nicola Savarese, *A Dictionary of Theatre Anthropology* (New York: Routledge, 1991), 33.

13. Lee Siegel, *Sacred and Profane Dimensions of Love in Indian Tradition: The Gitagovinda of Jayadeva* (New York: Oxford University Press, 1983), 55.

14. For example, see David R. Kinsley, *The Divine Player: A Study of Krsna Lila* (Delhi: Motilal Banarsidass, 1979).

15. For example, see the film *Holi, A Festival of Colour* (Princeton, NJ: Films for the Humanities and Sciences, 1999).

16. Frederique Apffel Marglin, "Refining the Body: Transformative Emotion in Ritual Dance," in *Divine Passions: The Social Construction of Emotion in India,* ed. Owen M. Lynch (Berkeley: University of California Press, 1990), 212–213.

17. "Toward an Anthropology of Self and Feeling," in *Culture Theory: Essays on Mind, Self, and Emotion,* ed. Richard A. Shweder and Robert A. Lavine (New York: Cambridge University Press, 1985), 137–157.

18. Marglin, 212.

19. "A Performative Approach to Ritual," *Proceedings of the British Academy* 65:113–169.

20. Marglin, 213.

21. Marglin, 233.

22. For example, see Frederique Apffel Marglin, *Wives of the God-King: The Rituals of the Devadasis of Puri* (New Delhi: Oxford University Press, 1985).

23. Marglin, "Refining the Body: Transformative Emotion in Ritual Dance," 224.

24. Ibid. See also Anne-Marie Gaston, *Bharata Natyam, From Temple to Theatre*, chapter 3, "The Sacred and Profane in Bharata Natyam" (New Delhi: Manohar Publishers & Distributors, 1996).

25. Ibid., 231.

26. Narayan, 8–9.

27. This was a corruption of *naach,* one of the many terms used to refer to dance; see Reginald Massey, *India's Kathak Dance, Past, Present and Future* (New Delhi: Abhinav Publications, 1999), 23.

28. Ibid.

29. Narayan, 23.

30. For example, see Massey, 43.

31. Phillip Zarrilli, *Kathakali Dance-Drama, Where Gods and Demons Come to Play* (New York: Routledge, 2000), 6.

32. For example, see ibid., and Sarah Caldwell, *Oh, Terrifying Mother: Sexuality, Violence and Worship of the Goddess Kali* (New York: Oxford University Press, 2001).

33. Phillip Zarrilli, "What Does It Mean to 'Become the Character': Power, Presence and Transcendence in Asian In-Body Disciplines of Practice," in *By Means of Performance: Intercultural Studies of Theatre and Ritual,* ed. Richard Schechner and Willa Appel (New York: Cambridge University Press, 1990), 131–133.

34. Ibid., 142.

35. Ibid., 144.

36. Andre Padoux, trans. Jacques Gontier, *Vac: The Concept of the Word in Selected Hindu Tantras* (Albany: State University of New York Press, 1990), 414.

37. Lewis Rowell, *Music and Musical Thought in Early India* (Chicago: University of Chicago, Press, 1992), 297.

38. For examples, see ibid., 298–301.

39. Ibid., 308–312.

40. Ibid., 328.

41. Ibid., 330.

42. Ibid., 331.

43. Ibid., 336.

44. Donna Marie Wulff, "On Practicing Religiously: Music as Sacred in India," in *Sacred Sound: Music in Religious Thought and Practice*, ed. Joyce Irwin (*JAAR Thematic Studies 50/1*), 150.

45. Ibid., 156.

46. Daniel M. Neuman, *The Life of Music in Northern India* (Chicago: The University of Chicago Press, 1990), 60–61.

47. Beryl De Zoete, *Other Mind: A Study of Dance in South India* (London: London Gollancz, 1953), 31.

48. See Rowell, 45.

49. Wulff, 154.

50. Wulff, 157–158.

51. Ananda K. Coomaraswamy, "Hindu View of Art: Theory of Beauty," in *The Dance of Shiva: Essays on Indian Art and Culture* (New York: Dover, 1985), 35–36.

4. TRANSFORMATIONS IN TIME AND SPACE

1. Anne-Marie Gaston, *Bharata Natyam: From Temple to Theatre* (New Delhi: Manohar Publishers & Distributors, 1996), 315–16.

2. Magdelene Gorringe, "Arangetram, Social Conventions and Artistic Endeavor," posted March 10, 2001 at www.Boloji.com, 3.

3. Kalpana Ram, "Dancing the Past Into Life: The *Rasa, Nritta* and *Raga* of Immigrant Existence," *The Australian Journal of Anthropology* 11(3) (2000): 262.

4. Ibid., 263.

5. Ibid.

6. Ibid., 266.

7. Ibid., 269.

8. Ibid., 270.

9. See Rustom Bharucha, *The Politics of Cultural Practice* (Hanover, NH: Wesleyan University Press, 2000) for an exploration of "secularism" in the Indian context. Not necessarily a rejection of religion as such, it has more to do, perhaps, with a more worldly approach to the divisions that religions have often supported.

10. Rustom Bharucha, *Chandralekha* (New Delhi: HarperCollins Publishers India Pvt. Ltd., 1995), 129.

11. Ibid., 130.

12. Bharucha, *The Politics of Cultural Practice,* 134.

13. Richard Schechner, "Rasaesthetics," in *TDR: The Drama Review* 45(3) (Fall 2001): 27–50.

14. Ibid., 29.

15. Ibid., 35.

16. Ibid., 32; see also Phillip Zarrilli, "What Does It Mean to 'Become the Character': Power, Presence and Transcendence in Asian In-Body Disciplines of Practice," in *By Means of Performance: Intercultural Studies of Theatre and Ritual,* ed. Richard Schechner and Willa Appel (New York: Cambridge University Press, 1990), 144.

Bibliography

Adams, Doug and Apostolos-Cappadona, Diane, eds. *Dance as Religious Studies.* New York: Crossroad Publishing Company, 1990.

Ananya. "Training in Indian Classical Dance: A Case Study." *Asian Theatre Journal* 13 (1) (Spring 1996: 68–91.

Antze, Rosemary Jeanes. "Teacher, Student, Language." *Parabola* 17 (3) (Fall 1992): 73–77.

Avanti, Meduri. "Bharatha Natyam—What Are You?" *Asian Theatre Journal* 5 (1) (1988): 1–22.

Barba, Eugenio and Savarese, Nicola. *A Dictionary of Theatre Anthropology: The Secret Art of the Performer.* Trans. Richard Fowler. New York: Routledge, 1991.

Beck, Guy L. *Sonic Theology: Hinduism and Sacred Sound.* Columbia: University of South Carolina Press, 1993.

Bharata-Muni. *The Natyashastra,* Vol. I and II. Trans. Manomohan Ghosh. Calcutta: Granthalaya Pvt. Ltd., 1967.

Bharucha, Rustom. *Chandralekha.* New Delhi: HarperCollins Publishers India Pvt. Ltd., 1995.

———. *The Politics of Cultural Practice.* Hanover, NH: Wesleyan University Press, 2000.

Clayton, Martin. *Time in Indian Music.* New York: Oxford University Press, 2000.

Coomaraswamy, Ananda K. *The Dance of Shiva: Essays on Indian Art and Culture.* New York: Dover, 1985.

———. *The Mirror of Gesture, Being the Abhinaya Darpana of Nandikeshvara.* 1917; reprint, New Delhi: Munshiram Manoharlal Publishers Pvt. Ltd., 1997.

———. *The Transformation of Nature in Art.* New Delhi: Munshiram Manoharlal Publishers Pvt. Ltd., 1974.

Coorlawala, Uttara Asha, et al. "Kapila Vatsyayan—Honorary Papers." *Dance Research Journal* 32 (1) (Summer 2000).

De, S. K. *Sanskrit Poetics as a Study of Aesthetic.* Berkeley: University of California Press, 1963.

De Zoete, Beryl. *Other Mind: A Study of Dance in South India.* London: London Gollancz, 1953.

Elgood, Heather. *Hinduism and the Religious Arts.* New York: Cassell, 1999.

Gargi, Balwant. *Theatre in India.* New York: Theatre Arts Books, 1962.

Gaston, Anne-Marie. *Bharata Natyam: From Temple to Theatre.* New Delhi: Manohar Publishers & Distributors, 1996.

Gorringe, Magdelene. "Arangetram, Social Conventions and Artistic Endeavor." www.Boloji.com, March 10, 2001.

Haas, George C. O. *The Dasharupa: A Treatise on Hindu Dramaturgy by Dhanamjaya.* Delhi: Motilal Banarsidass, 1962.

Highwater, Jamake. *Dance: Rituals of Experience.* New York: Oxford University Press, 1978.

Ingalls, Daniel H., Jeffrey Masson, Moussaieff, and M. V. Patwardhan, trans. *The Dhvanyaloka of Anandavardhana with the Locana of Abhinavagupta.* Cambridge: Harvard University Press, 1990.

Irwin, Joyce. *Sacred Sound: Music in Religious Thought and Practice.* Chico, CA: Scholars Press, 1983.

Iyer, K. Bharatha. *Kathakali.* New Delhi: Munshiram Manoharlal Publishers Pvt. Ltd., 1983.

Katyal, Anjum. "Performing the Goddess: Sacred Ritual Into Professional Performance." *TDR: The Drama Review* 45 (Spring 2001): 96–117.

Kersenboom, Saskia C. *Nityasumangali: Devadasi Tradition in South India.* Delhi: Motilal Banarsidass Publishers Pvt. Ltd., 1987.

——. *Word, Sound, Image: The Life of a Tamil Text.* Washington, DC: Berg Publishers, 1995.

Khare, R. S., ed. *The Eternal Food: Gastronomic Ideas and Experiences of Hindus and Buddhists.* Albany: State University of New York Press, 1992.

Kinsley, David R. *Hinduism: A Cultural Perspective.* 2nd ed. Englewood Cliffs, NJ: Prentice Hall, 1993.

——. *The Divine Player: A Study of Krsna Lila.* Delhi: Motilal Banarsidass, 1979.

Klinger, George, ed. *Bharata Natyam in Cultural Perspective.* New Delhi: Manohar, American Institute of Indian Studies, 1993.

Kothari, Dr. Sunil and Bimal Mukherjee, eds. *Rasa: The Indian Performing Arts in the Last Twenty-five Years.* Calcutta: Anamika Kala Sangam Research and Publications, 1991.

Kramrisch, Stella. *The Presence of Siva.* Princeton: Princeton University Press, 1981.

Kyer, K. Bharatha. *Kathakali: The Sacred Dance-Drama of Malabar.* New Delhi: Oriental Books Reprint Corporation, 1983.

Lakshmi, C. S. *The Singer and the Song.* New Delhi: Kali for Women, 2000.

Lannoy, Richard. *The Speaking Tree: A Study of Indian Culture and Society.* New York: Oxford University Press, 1971.

Leslie, Julia, ed. *Roles and Rituals for Hindu Women.* London: Pinter Publishers, 1991.

Lopez, Donald S., Jr. *Religions of India in Practice.* Princeton: Princeton University Press, 1995.

Lutgendorf, Philip. *The Life of a Text.* Berkeley: University of California Press, 1991.

Lynch, Owen M., ed. *Divine Passions: The Social Construction of Emotion in India.* Berkeley: University of California Press, 1990.

Mahony, William K. *The Artful Universe: An Introduction to the Vedic Religious Imagination.* Albany: State University of New York Press, 1998.

Maitra, Romain. "The Dancer's Dilemma." *UNESCO Courier* 49 (1) (Jan. 1996): 36–39.

Malamoud, Charles. *Cooking the World: Ritual and Thought in Ancient India.* Trans. David White. New York: Oxford University Press, 1996.

Malik, S. C., ed. *Dhvani, Nature and Culture of Sound.* Delhi: Indira Gandhi National Centre for the Arts, 1991.

Marglin, Frederique Apffel. *Wives of the God-King: The Rituals of the Devadasis of Puri.* New Delhi: Oxford University Press, 1985.

Marranca, Bonnie and Gautam Dasgupta, eds. *Interculturalism and Performance.* New York: PAJ Publications, 1991.

Massey, Reginald. *India's Kathak Dance, Past, Present, Future.* New Delhi: Abhinav Publications, 1999.

Meister, Michael W., ed. *Cooking for the Gods.* Philadelphia: University of Pennsylvania Press, 1995.

Miller, Barbara Stoler. "Moving Designs of Masked Emotion." *Parabola* 6 (3) (1987): 85–89.

Miller, Barbara Stoler, ed. *The Plays of Kalidasa, Theater of Memory.* New York: Columbia University Press, 1984.

——. *The Powers of Art: Patronage in Indian Culture.* New York: Oxford University Press, 1992.

Nair, D. Appukuttan and K. Ayyappa Paniker, eds. *Kathakali: The Art of the Non-Worldly.* Bombay: Marg Publications, 1995.

Nair, Savitry. "Hands that Speak Volumes." *UNESCO Courier* 46 (9) (Sept. 1993): 34–37.

Narayanan, Vasudha. "Diglossic Hinduism: Liberation and Lentils." *Journal of the American Academy of Religion* 68 (4) (2000): 761–779.

Neuman, Daniel M. *The Life of Music in Northern India.* Chicago: University of Chicago Press, 1990.

O'Flaherty, Wendy Doniger. *Dreams, Illusions and Other Realities.* Chicago: University of Chicago Press, 1984.

Orr, Leslie C. *Donors, Devotees, and Daughters of God.* New York: Oxford University Press, 2000.

O'Shea, Janet. "'Traditional' Indian Dance and the Making of Interpretive Communities." *Asian Theatre Journal* 15 (1) (Spring 1998): 45–63.

Pal, Pratapaditya, ed. *Dancing to the Flute.* Australia: The Art Gallery of New South Wales, 1997.

Panchal, Goverdhan. *The Theatres of Bharata and Some Aspects of Sanskrit Play-production.* New Delhi: Munshiram Manoharlal Publishers Pvt. Ltd., 1996.

Pande, Anupa. *The Natyashastra Tradition and Ancient Indian Society.* Jodhpur: Kusumanjali Prakashan, 1993.

Parthasarathy, R., trans. *The Cilappatikaram of Ilanko Atikal.* New York: Columbia University Press, 1993.

Pesch, Ludwig. *The Illustrated Guide to South Indian Classical Music.* New Delhi: Oxford University Press, 1999.

Ram, Kalpana. "Dancing the Past Into Life: The *Rasa, Nrtta* and *Raga* of Immigrant Existence." *The Australian Journal of Anthropology* 11 (3) (2000): 261–273.

——. "Listening to the Call of Dance: Rethinking Authenticity Essentialism." *The Australian Journal of Anthropology* 11 (3) (2000): 358–364.

Rao, Suvarnalata, Wim van der Meer, and Jane Harvey. *The Raga Guide.* Ed. Joep Bor. Nimbus Records, printed in the U.K. by Zenith Media (UK) Limited, 1999.

Richmond, Farley P., Darius L. Swann, and Philip B. Zarrilli. *Indian Theatre: Traditions of Performance.* Honolulu: University of Hawaii Press, 1990.

Rowell, Lewis. *Music and Musical Thought in Early India.* Chicago: University of Chicago Press, 1992.

Roy, Arundhati. *The God of Small Things.* New York: Random House, 1997.

Sarabhai, Mrinalini. *Creations.* New York: Mapin International, 1986.

Sax, William S. *Dancing the Self: Personhood and Performance in the Pandav Lila of Garhwal.* New York: Oxford University Press, 2002.

——. *The Gods at Play: Lila in South Asia.* New York: Oxford University Press, 1995.

Schechner, Richard. *Performance Studies: An Introduction.* New York: Routledge, 2002.

——. *Performance Theory.* New York: Routledge, 1977.

——. "Rasaesthetics." *TDR: The Drama Review* 45 (3) (2001): 27–50.

——. *The Future of Ritual.* New York: Routledge, 1995.

Schechner, Richard and Willa Appel, eds. *By Means of Performance: Intercultural Studies of Theatre and Ritual.* New York: Cambridge University Press, 1990.

Sethi, Rajeev, et al. *Aditi: The Living Arts of India.* Washington, DC: Smithsonian Institution Press, 1985.

Shankar, Ravi. *My Music, My Life.* New York: Simon and Schuster, 1968.

——. *Raga Mala.* Ed. George Harrison. New York: Welcome Rain Publishers, 1999.

Sharma, Arvind, ed. *The Little Clay Cart.* Albany: State University of New York Press, 1994.

Shattan, Merchant-Prince. *Manimekhalaii.* Trans. Alain Danielou. New York: New Directions, 1989.

Shweder, Richard A. and Robert A. Lavine, eds. *Culture Theory: Essays on Mind, Self, and Emotion.* New York: Cambridge University Press, 1985.

Siegel, Lee. *Fires of Love: Waters of Peace*. Honolulu: University of Hawaii Press, 1983.

Singer, Milton. *When a Great Tradition Modernizes*. New York: Praeger Publishers, 1972.

Singh, Shanta Serbjeet, ed. *Indian Dance: The Ultimate Metaphor*. Chicago: Art Media Ltd., 2000.

Subramaniam, V. *The Sacred and the Secular in India's Performing Arts*. New Delhi: Ashish Publishing House, 1980.

Thielmann, Selina. *Sounds of the Sacred Religious Music in India*. New Delhi: A.P.H. Publishing Corporation, 1998.

Turner, Victor. *From Ritual to Theatre: The Human Seriousness of Play*. New York: PAJ Publications, 1982.

Varadpande, M. L. *History of Indian Theatre, Loka Ranga, Panorama of Indian Folk Theatre*. New Delhi: Shakti Malik, Abhinav Publications, 1992.

Vatsyayan, Kapila. *Classical Indian Dance in Literature and the Arts*. New Delhi: Sangeet Natak Akademi, 1968.

——. *Indian Classical Dance*. New Delhi: Director, Publications Division, Ministry of Information and Broadcasting, Government of India, 1992.

——. *Bharata, The Natyashastra*. New Delhi: Sahitya Akademi, 1996.

Wade, Bonnie C. *Imaging Sounds*. Chicago: University of Chicago Press, 1998.

——. *Music in India, The Classical Traditions*. Rev. ed. New Delhi: Manohar Publishers and Distributers, 1999.

Waterhouse, David, ed. *Dance of India*. Mumbai: Popular Prakashan, 1998.

Wulff, Donna M. "Religion in a New Mode: The Convergence of the Aesthetic and the Religious in Medieval India." *Journal of the American Academy of Religion* LIV (4): 673–688.

Younger, Paul. *The Home of the Dancing Sivan*. New York: Oxford University Press, 1995.

Zarrilli, Phillip B. *Kathakali Dance-Drama: Where Gods and Demons Come to Play*. New York: Routledge, 2000.

——. *When the Body Becomes All Eyes*. Delhi: Oxford University Press, 1998.

Zimmer, Heinrich. *Myths and Symbols in Indian Art and Civilization*. Ed. Joseph Campbell. Princeton: Princeton University Press, 1974.

INDIAN PERFORMING ARTS ON VIDEOTAPE—VHS NTSC FORMAT

Circles Cycles: Kathak Dance. VHS. Produced and directed by Robert Gottlieb. Berkeley, CA: University of California Extension Media Center, 1989.

Given to Dance: India's Odissi Tradition. VHS. Madison, WI: Film Distribution Office, Center for South Asian Studies, 1986.

Great Tales in Asian Art. VHS. West Long Branch, NJ: Kultur, 1995.

Holi, A Festival of Colour. A Stein Film production in cooperation with SCPS. Produced by Michael Duffy. Researched and directed by Robyn Beeche. Princeton, NJ: Films for the Humanities and Sciences, 1999.

The JVC Video Anthology of World Music and Dance: South Asia I. VHS. Produced by JVC,
    Victor Company of Japan, Tokyo, 1988. Cambridge, MA: Rounder Records, 1990.

The JVC Video Anthology of World Music and Dance: South Asia II. VHS. Produced by JVC,
    Victor Company of Japan, Tokyo, 1988. Cambridge, MA: Rounder Records, 1990.

The JVC Video Anthology of World Music and Dance: Book IV. VHS. Produced by JVC, Vic-
    tor Company of Japan, Tokyo; Cambridge, MA: Rounder Records, 1990.

Kalakshetra. VHS. Produced by Adam Clapham for Griffin Productions. Boulder, CO:
    Centre Productions, 1985.

Raga. VHS. A Deben Bhattacharya production. Guildford, CT: Audio-Forum, Distribu-
    tor, 1969.

Raga/Ravi Shankar. VHS. New York: Mystic Fire Video, 1991.

Rhythms to Nirvana. VHS. Princeton, NJ: Films for the Humanities and Sciences, 1999.

Taking a Ride on the Clay Cart: Dynamics of Sanskrit Theatre. VHS. Production casebook
    by Betty Bernhard and Kailash Pandya. Staten Island, NY: Insight Media, 1993.

Zarrilli, Phillip B. *Introduction to Kathakali Dance-Drama.* VHS. New York: Routledge,
    2000.

——. *The Killing of Kirmira (Kirmira Vadham).* VHS. New York: Routledge, 2000.

Index